Riding TANDEM

LEANING into the LEADING of GOD

Annie Pajcic

THOUARTEXALTED, INC.

Creating Art through God's Word

www.thouartexalted.com

TABLE OF CONTENTS

WEEKS OF STUDY

1. WEEK ONE: Time for Takeoff

18th Video

2. WEEK TWO: Alignment

3. WEEK THREE: Necessary Stops

4. WEEK FOUR: Don't Stop Pedaling

5. WEEK FIVE: Enjoy the Ride

6. WEEK SIX: Mark the Moments

Let me begin by saying THANK YOU for purchasing Riding Tandem. Whether you are doing this Bible study alone or with a group of friends, I hope this guide will be helpful to you.

Riding Tandem is a six-week Bible study divided into the T-A-N-D-E-M acronym: **T**-ime for Takeoff, **A**-lignment, **N**-ecessary Stops, **D**-on't Stop Pedaling, **E**-njoy the Ride, and **M**-ark the Moments. The lessons are divided into five segments of homework that should take no longer than 30 minutes a day. If you are a small group leader, have a highlighter nearby to highlight the questions that mean the most to you during your quiet times. There are also "tandem icons" that point to the more personal questions. Your highlights and the tandem icons will be a quick reference for discussion when leading your small group.

Videos: I encourage you to view the teaching video following each week's lesson. Videos are available at **www.thouartexalted.com/riding-tandem.**

I believe the purpose of a small group is to have fellowship with one another and grow in the knowledge of God's Word. I love small groups because they build friendships that allow the Word to penetrate into the realness of our lives. After leading small groups for years, I have some TIPS to share with you:

1. Keep track of TIME.
Decide ahead of time how long your group sessions will be. If you choose to watch the video, add 35 minutes. For small group discussion time, take the time allotted and divide by the days of homework (in this case, five). For example: If you have 50 minutes to discuss homework, then allow 10 minutes of discussion per day. Use your highlighted and tandem questions as your main focus. If you have time, ask your group if one of the questions stood out among the others and how God used that question to make a difference in their life. Remember to always look at your watch and keep the conversation going. If you have time at the end, you can always go back to look at a question.

2. Keep conversation on TOPIC.
Women can be easily distracted and quickly get off course. Your job is to keep everyone on track. Ask the Holy Spirit to give you gentleness as you steer the conversation back on topic.

3. Keep TALKY people to a minimum.
Not everyone wants to share in a small group. Allow a chance for everyone to participate and be careful that no one person dominates the conversation. If you have this situation, you might want to gently speak to her in private and encourage her to allow others to share their answers. Be sensitive to the needs of others and ask God for wisdom.

4. Allow TIME to prepare.
As a leader, be prepared to facilitate your small group. This means … do your homework! You can't lead if you haven't taken time to sit with the Lord and study Riding Tandem.

5. TAKE time to PRAY with and for your small group.
This is one of the most important aspects of your group. I would encourage you to take prayer requests at the end of each discussion time and emphasize the confidentiality of the group. Prayers and discussions are personal and should not be taken outside your small group.

This is not a complete list of "how-to" lead a small group by any means, but hopefully it hit on a few good points! Remember to be real. Be yourself. Be inviting. Allow the Holy Spirit to lead you as you have the privilege to lead your small group. And, if you ever have any questions, please e-mail me at apajcic@thouartexalted.com.

We are praying for you!

Have you ever ridden a tandem bicycle?

Growing up, our family had a tan and white striped tandem. Oh, the beauty of a bicycle built for two! Yet because our family was built for six, seats were limited. At the age of seven, I could barely reach the pedals AND hold on to the handlebars at the same time. I found out early on that it was easier to let one of my sisters take the front seat and do **all** the work. I was along for the ride and glad for it.

Honestly, my family had good reason not to trust my biking abilities. While I would not describe Jacksonville as a "hilly" town, there is one place where you can feel the slight downhill tilt of the road. The combination of this hill, a parked car, my distraction, and the front end of my banana seat bicycle was not good. BOOM. You can only imagine.

Fortunately, **Riding Tandem** is not about how many accidents we have had. It is not about climbing the ranks of the seating chart, reaching for the pedals, or navigating parked cars. **Riding Tandem** is about an authentic, everyday, one-on-one relationship with God. It's about learning our position on the back of the bike and trusting God with the front steering. Our personal relationship with God is built for two. He is the Captain, so we must learn to lean into His leading, pedal forward, and trust Him with the directions. **Riding Tandem** will teach us that while our final destination is heaven, our destiny on earth has purpose. We are not just along for the ride. We are **a part** of the ride. God wants us to live an abundant life completely surrendered to His leading. **Riding Tandem** with Jesus is letting go of the handlebars and experiencing His power as we pedal. Everyday.

Riding Tandem is divided into six chapters using the acronym **T-A-N-D-E-M.**

> Week One: **T**-ime for Takeoff
> Week Two: **A**-lignment
> Week Three: **N**-ecessary Stops
> Week Four: **D**-on't Stop Pedaling
> Week Five: **E**-njoy the Ride
> Week Six: **M**-ark the Moments

Each day we have a choice to make. Are we going to steer our own stories, or are we going to allow God to guide? My prayer for us as we journey through **Riding Tandem** is that we will hop on the back and allow God to take the wheel. He is our teacher and life is our classroom. If we have teachable hearts, God will use our stories in tandem with His Word *like* to teach us His principles. Yes, it can be hard. Sometimes it feels easier to be in control, work hard, and get the job done. *LAT* But God has a bigger plan. His ways are higher than ours and always better. Where is God taking you today? Are you equipped for the ride? He promises never to leave your side as the Captain of your life. Do you trust His leading? Are you willing to let go of the handlebars? Allow me to pray this prayer as we begin the journey of **Riding Tandem.**

*Dear Lord, today I choose to hop on the back seat of the tandem. I choose to let You steer the story of my life and teach me the lessons ahead. Life is Your classroom, and I am Your student. I will take the time to sit, listen, study hard, and do my work. I will pedal hard and learn to trust in Your teaching. While I can't see the road ahead, You can. I know that You go before me. I know there will be times when I am afraid and want to clutch on to my handlebars and take control. Please remind me that You are right there with me. You will never leave me. At times, I might want You to speed things up, and at other times, slow life down. Remind me that Your timing and pace are perfect. We are in this ride **together**. With You as my Captain, I can press on, be patient, and persevere with joy. Climb on sweet Lord! Balance the bike for me so I can take the position as Your co-captain. Lead me in the way everlasting so that I may soar in Your presence. It's time to ride. Amen.*

It's a beautiful day for a bike ride!
Lots of love and grace,

Lesson One / TIME FOR TAKEOFF

Imagine a tandem bicycle has just arrived at your back door. Immediately you notice the note tied to the front handlebar.

Welcome! Let Me introduce Myself. My name is Captain, and I am overjoyed that you chose Me to ride through life with you. We are going to take amazing adventures together. As your Captain, I know the direction we will take. There's no need to be distracted by all the latest gadgets and gizmos because I have all the equipment you need. I have plenty of water, and rest stops are planned well in advance. If you ever feel tired, insecure, or winded, just stop pedaling and coast. I have you in the palm of My hand. If you ever get scared, worried, or doubt My leading, just lean in and trust that I am steering you in the right direction. Make sure to mark the special moments we will have together and always remember to enjoy the ride. Life can get tricky sometimes, but if you trust Me, I will give you eyes to see from My perspective. Do not worry. As your Captain, I am in full control. Before you climb aboard, please read My instructions and know your seating assignment. It is very important to know our takeoff procedures before we ride together on this tandem bicycle.

With everlasting love,
Your Captain

It's **T-ime for Takeoff!** The tandem bicycle will be our visual focus for **Riding Tandem.** Take a look at this illustration and soak in the imagery.

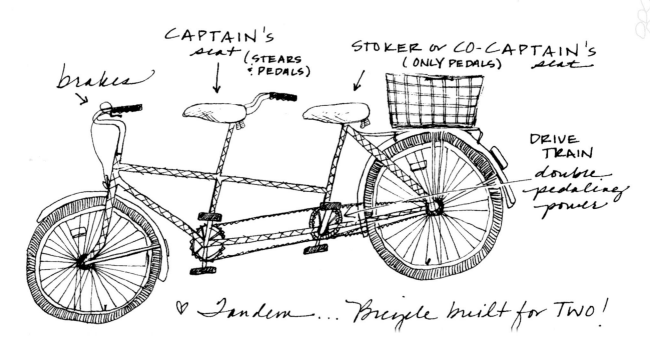

For the next six weeks, our transportation of choice is the tandem bicycle. Before we take off though, we need to be familiar with **takeoff procedures** and following instructions. Both are very important for takeoff. **Any takeoff.**

I boarded the plane and sat in my assigned seat that just happened to be located in the emergency aisle. The flight attendant, who seemed a little skittish, anxiously asked me if I felt responsible enough to handle **an emergency situation**, if one was to occur. "Absolutely," I said with confidence as I scanned the little white box above my head that said, **"Pull-Down."**

If she hadn't been so freaky about my ability to be responsible, I probably would not have had so many waves of doubt rush into my brain. But rush they did. And fast.

What if I were asked to execute an emergency procedure?
What if I had to open that little white box above my head?
Could I handle an emergency situation? I mean, I was only 21-years-old.

Even though my whole body was saying, *"NO! Don't touch the white box,"* my hand began to move upward. My fingers barely touched the little white box when the outer cover popped open. I was horrified. Instantly, I could feel the glaring eyes of the flight attendant as she walked in my direction. This was it. I was going to be kicked off the island.

"What have you done? You have tampered with the emergency box! Now we will be late for departure because of— **YOU**. Call the technician! We have an emergency. We cannot takeoff until we reattach the little white box."

I was ready for handcuffs.

None were needed. My punishment was 150 irritated, frustrated, and irate passengers staring at me. Curiosity not only killed the cat, it killed my desire to EVER tamper with takeoff procedures again. **Ever.**

Following instructions, God's instructions, is our T-ime (preparation) for Takeoff. Tampering with His instructions not only delays our departure, but also irritates those around us. I learned this the hard way!

Seating positions are also important for takeoff. As you can see from the illustration, it is very clear this bicycle is built for **two**. The front rider is called the captain. The captain's job is to steer the bike **and** pedal. The back rider is called the stoker or co-captain whose **only job** is to pedal. Slowly re-read those sentences and carefully look at the words AND and ONLY. I hope you are beginning to see a creative connection with our seating position on the tandem bike. God is our Captain, and He is on the front seat to steer and pedal. Yes, ladies, this means we are on the back seat and can **only** pedal. As hard as this might seem (not to be in control and steer this tandem journey), God is best suited for the position of Captain.

The word for captain can also be translated: **master**. The Greek word for master is **"kyrios,"** meaning Lord, and it is used more than 740 times in the New Testament, usually referring to Jesus. I love that kyrios is defined as **one who has the power**. It is a title of honor, respect, and reverence. It also refers to the one to whom a person belongs.[1] Kyrios was often defined as "the relationship between Jesus and those who believed in him as Christ: Jesus was their Lord and Master who was to be served with all their hearts."[2] When we place our trust in Jesus, He becomes our Savior as well as our Captain— the ONE WHO HAS THE POWER. (And, the driver's seat!)

Now that we understand more about the word used for captain, it's time to ask a very important question: **Why is Jesus a good Captain? Let's begin!**

Read the following verses and write down the qualifications of Jesus as our Captain in each passage.

- **Philippians 2:9-11**

_____
_____
_____

- **Romans 10:9-13**

_____
_____

- **John 14:6**

_____

_____

_____

- **John 13:12-17**

_____

_____

_____

- **Colossians 1:15-20**

_____

_____

_____

Jesus is MORE than qualified to hire as your Captain! Be creative and fill out this job application **for Jesus** based on the verses you just read. Have fun sharing these in your small group. *Please note: When you see a tandem icon, this is a great question to ponder as a small group.*

riding TANDEM — job application

Position applying for: _____

Name: ___JESUS_____ Phone Number: _____ E-Mail: _____

Address: _____ References: _____

_____

Recent Employment: _____ How long have you been employed in this position?_____

Describe your qualifications for this position including education, skills, abilities, and work experience.

_____
_____
_____
_____
_____
_____

Describe why you are applying for this position.

_____
_____
_____

Have you ever been convicted of a crime? Have you ever been arrested? Explain.

_____
_____
_____

Can we contact you at work? Yes:_____ No: _____ When are you available? _____

Signature: _____ Date:_____

We can see with clarity that Jesus, **the kyrios**—*the One who has the power,* is best suited for the job as our front seat driver. Our Captain is the Lord Jesus. Every knee will bow one day to recognize this powerful truth. Confession in His name alone has the power to save us. He is the way, the truth, and the life. He is our Teacher. He is Lord. His name alone is a title of honor, respect, and reverence. He is also a humble servant. He is the image of the invisible God, and **all** of God's fullness dwells in Him. He is the Creator and Sustainer. He is the beginning of all things, holds everything together, and made peace for all things through His blood shed on the cross (Colossians 1:15-20).

This lesson is KEY to prepare for takeoff. In fact, I'm lifting off my seat right now just having read our Captain's job application! Jesus is our Captain, and His job on this tandem ride is to steer, pedal, and **lead.** If you are in an emergency situation, He **wants** you to pull down the little white box. He's got the power to steer you in the right direction and is ready to give you grace—not to stare you down, humiliate you, and expose your mess-ups.

Tomorrow, we will discuss our role in the seating position as the stoker and co-captain. I can hardly wait. Great job today!

Lesson Two/ GET STOKED!

Yesterday, we learned that Jesus is well-qualified to be our Captain in this tandem ride called life.

Today, we are going to discuss our positioning on this bicycle built for two. It is important to note again that the back rider, called the co-captain or stoker, **only** pedals. We are not called to steer. I know this is tough news for some of us or maybe all of us. It's not easy hopping on the back. Why? We want to be in charge. We want the control seat where we can make the calls and call the shots. But in God's economy, this is **not** our position. Our position is on the back.

Look up the following verses and answer the questions. What repeating word prepares us to be co-captains and stokers with Jesus as our Captain? What is God's response when we take this position?

Repeating Word/ God's Response

• **1 Peter 5:5-6**

_____/_____
_____/_____
_____/_____

• **James 4:10**

_____/_____
_____/_____
_____/_____

• **Psalm 25:9**

_____/_____
_____/_____
_____/_____

• **Matthew 23:12**

_____/_____
_____/_____
_____/_____

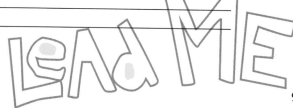

Humility is the opposite of pride. The position of pride wants the power and prestige of the Captain's seat. But God's Word makes it clear that "pride goes before destruction" (Proverbs 16:18). When we are humble enough to move to the rear, God guides and teaches us what is right. When we clothe ourselves in humility, God responds with grace. When we humble ourselves, God **lifts us up**. Humility will always instruct us how to lean on the Captain's leading. No more backseat driving, girls. Keep pedaling and **leave the steering to God.**

Did you notice on the illustration that the co-captain is also called a **stoker?** A stoker is a term meaning: a laborer employed to tend and fuel a furnace, especially a furnace that generates steam, as on a steamship or a person who pedals on the back of a tandem bicycle.[3]

To stoke means: to stir or add to the fire.

Read 2 Timothy 1:6-7 and get stoked! (Sorry, I couldn't resist. Stoked is slang for "get pumped up!")

What is Paul telling us to do?

_____

_____

_____

_____

_____

Paul is reminding young Timothy—and us—to stir up or **fan into flames** the gifts God has given. This stirring can be used in terms of being strengthened physically or inflaming one's mind as a fire is kindled anew or lighted up.[4]

This is incredible! Over the next six weeks, we will learn that our position on this tandem bike is on the **back. We are the stokers**. We are in charge of tending the furnace that generates power for us to pedal. This power comes not from pride or our own personal efforts to pedal, but from our humility as we learn to trust in the Source, the Lord, our Kyrios. Tending the fire is spending time with God, building a one-on-one relationship, spreading His Word, and serving Him with our gifts. This is preparation for **T-ime for Takeoff** at its core. *The Message* translation of 2 Timothy 1:7 reminds us to keep the special gifts of ministry that God has given us **ablaze!**

" . . . —keep that ablaze! God doesn't want us to be shy with his gifts, but bold and loving and sensible."

I am not sure if the band Unspoken used Eugene Peterson's version of 2 Timothy 1:6-7, but I do know it was not a coincidence that I heard their song: Let Your Light Shine on the radio. Read the lyrics and see if you get goose bumps like I did!

This world can be cold and bitter
Feels like we're in the dead of winter
Waiting on something better
But am I really gonna hide forever?

Over and over again
I hear Your voice in my head
Let Your light shine, let Your light shine for all to see

(Chorus)
Start a fire in my soul
Fan the flame and make it grow
So there's no doubt or denying

Let it burn so brightly
That everyone around can see
That it's You, that it's You that we need
Start a fire in me[5]

God wants to start a fire of faith in each one of us. Sometimes, we can feel like life is cold and bitter. Gripping for control, we tighten our hands on the handlebars until our knuckles turn white. Today, if you are struggling with an area of control, give it to Jesus. He's got the credentials to set you free.

Be humble and stoke the fire within you. Fan the flame. Let your light shine for all the world to see.

Your Captain is waiting.

Read John 8:12. In light of today's lesson, what do you think this verse teaches you as you learn to ride tandem with Him? Where do you need to let go of control?

_____

_____

_____

_____

_____

Lord, You are the Light of the world. You are the Light that gives my life purpose and power. I pray I would fan into flames the gifts You have given to me. With humility, I pray to surrender my pride and learn my position on the back seat. Teach me to give You the control seat as I lean into Your leading. I am a stoker! This special relationship shows my commitment to serve You, honor You, trust You, believe in You, and ride through life with You. This tandem journey was meant for two—You and Me. I am honored to be Your co-captain. I will take the next six weeks to learn from You as You lead me in the right direction. Show me how I can use my gifts to light the fire of passion within me and others. Teach me to ride tandem with You. Amen.

Lesson Three / KNOWING IS BELIEVING

Look back at our bicycle illustration. How many people can ride on a tandem? That's right! The tandem is built for two. Not three or four.

Our relationship with Jesus is a **personal one**. While it is important to have fellowship, prayer partners, a good church home, and mentors, we must make time for Jesus one-on-one in order to **know** Him.

T-ime for Takeoff is about developing this personal relationship. As women with busy lives, and I am sure you have one, we need to grow **deeper** in our relationship with the Lord. But how do we do this?

How do we worry less and praise more?

_____

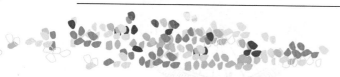

How do we surrender our plans and let God steer?

_____

How do we become less self-centered and more Christ-focused?

_____

How can we connect with Christ on a day-to-day personal level?

_____

As BUSYNESS tends to drive our lives, we need an authentic connection with our Captain. I believe our first step towards building a deeper relationship with Jesus is **knowing** who He is and **why** we believe in Him. We need to be 100% confident in His position as our Captain.

What is the result when we have confidence in the Lord?

- **Jeremiah 17:7-8**

_____
_____
_____

- **Hebrews 4:16**

_____
_____
_____

- **1 John 5:13-15**

_____
_____
_____

Confidence in our Captain deepens our faith so we do not fear when trouble comes, we stay faithful when we get doubtful, and we continue to believe even when life is hard. Confidence in Christ allows us to approach God with boldness knowing He hears our prayers and answers them according to His will. The apostle Paul was passionate about having this confidence. In his letter to the church at Colosse, Paul encourages us not to give into doubt, but **believe with certainty** that Jesus is the truth. Paul was a true-hearted stoker!

Today, be filled with confidence as you read Colossians 2:2-4. Fill in this personal prayer.

"_____ (your name) I want you to be encouraged and knit together by strong ties of love. _____ (your name), I want you to have **complete confidence** that you understand God's mysterious plan, which is Christ himself. In him lie hidden **all** the treasures of wisdom and knowledge. I am telling you this so no one will deceive you, _____ (your name), with well-crafted arguments."

Paul's mission is stoking the fire of Jesus so we can be **confident** and **encouraged** in Him. Paul is pedaling with intention to keep the power source aflame. He wants nothing more than for us to understand that true wisdom and knowledge are revealed when we believe in the richest treasure of all. **Jesus.**

Let me ask you a pivotal question.

> **Who is Jesus to you? Be honest. Share a time when you trusted Him to be your Captain and steer your life.**

_____
_____
_____
_____
_____

Read Matthew 16:13-17 and answer the following questions.

> **What is the first question Jesus asks His disciples? What is their answer?**

_____
_____

> **What is the second question Jesus asks? What is Peter's answer?**

_____
_____

> **Who revealed this mystery to Peter?**

_____

Peter confesses Jesus is the Messiah, the Son of the Living God. Peter is confessing with **confidence** that Jesus is his Captain. He is proclaiming Jesus is his Kyrios, the One to whom he belongs. If you remember from day one's lesson, kyrios is about a relationship. As we prepare for our journey together in **Riding Tandem**, we must define this relationship if we want a deeper connection with our Captain. **Who do you say Jesus is?**

Is He just a good man? Is He just a good teacher? Or, is He the Christ, the son of the Living God? Do you really **know** Him?

When we declare Jesus is the Christ, we are confessing (among many things) that Jesus is our Captain. He has the power to steer our lives, and we **trust** without a doubt that He is leading us in the right direction. I love the following quote from Liz Curtis Higgs: "Believing in God is easy. Trusting in God is hard." Why? Because we do not like surrendering the control! Until we know Jesus personally, we will not trust Him. But how can we be certain that we can trust Him?

> "Those who know your name trust in you, for you, O LORD, have never abandoned anyone who searches for you."
> Psalm 9:10 (NLT)

> **Why can we trust Him according to Psalm 9:10?**

_____
_____
_____

Believing Jesus is the Christ, the Son of the Living God, is foundational to the Christian faith and an essential element in our journey of **Riding Tandem**. You are not going to TRUST someone to captain your life if you do not KNOW Him personally. The word used here for "know" is *yada*. It means: to learn to know, to perceive, to know by experience, to recognize, to be revealed.[5] Knowing Jesus is your Captain is believing and **trusting** He will never abandon you. Knowing Jesus is experiencing a one-on-one relationship with Him. He loves you and desires a deeper connection. He wants to reveal Himself to you. Knowing is believing. **Believing is trusting.**

What I love about the Christian faith is that even though God already knows every hair on our head, He waits for **our invitation** to believe in Him. He waits for us to **invite Him** into our hearts. He will never force us to move to the back seat. It is our decision to make Him Captain and to follow Him.

Read Revelation 3:20. What does this tell you about a personal relationship with Jesus?

_____

_____

Jesus is standing and waiting. It is our **confession** in Jesus that opens the door to eternal life (Romans 10:9-13). Our belief that He is the Christ, the son of the Living God, is the beginning of an abundant bike ride. The Creator of the universe is waiting for us to **know** Him—so He can reveal Himself to us in a personal, experiential, one-on-one relationship.

Finish by reading Paul's prayer in **Colossians 2:6-7** from _The Message_ and be encouraged!

"And now, _____ (your name), just as you accepted Christ Jesus as your Lord, you must continue **to follow him.** Let your roots grow down into him, and let your life be built on him. Then your faith, _____ (your name), will grow strong in the truth you were taught, and you will overflow with thankfulness. I want you, _____ (your name) woven into a tapestry of love, in touch with everything there is to know of God. Then you, _____ (your name), will have a mind confident and at rest, **focused** on Christ, God's great mystery. All the richest treasures of wisdom and knowledge are embedded in that mystery and nowhere else. And you, _____ (your name), have been shown the mystery!"

What a great day! We must continue to fan the flames and follow Christ. Dig your roots deep. Build your life on Him. Be confident that He is leading you! You are woven in the tapestry of His love with a passion so deep you can rest in His peace that surpasses human understanding. He has your life on a perfect path, on a perfect timeline, going the **perfect speed.** Amen.

Lesson Four EARS TO HEAR, EYES TO SEE

During the past three days, we have learned who our Captain is and why He has the authority to take the front seat.

We have learned our position on the back seat and the truth that knowing Him personally opens the door to confident belief and trust. Today, we will look at why it's important to prepare our hearts **before** we ride with God through our day. **We need eyes to see and ears to hear in order to lean into His leading.** Recently, God showed me a life verse we should all tape to our refrigerators! Isaiah 50:4 opens with these words, "Sovereign Lord." The word, sovereign, is translated _Adonai_, where God is addressed submissively and with reverence. It is similar to our Greek word for Master or kyrios. It is like saying Lord, Lord with **double** emphasis. Double the speed. **Double the pedaling power.**

"The Sovereign Lord has taught me what to say, so that I can strengthen the weary. Every morning he makes me eager to hear what he is going to teach me."
Isaiah 50:4 (GW)

Slowly read Isaiah 50:4. Why should we spend time with God every morning?

_____

_____

_____

According to Isaiah 50:4, when we acknowledge that our Captain is Lord, Lord, we are addressing our God with reverence and given words to say that strengthen the weary. I don't know about you, but I want to be first in line to receive wise words that give hope to my children and joy to my friends. I bet you might be in line, too, perhaps to give encouragement to your husband or loved ones. Better yet, what an awesome day when we can remember God's promises to give **us** a boost when we find ourselves in circumstances we were not expecting.

I was in a coffee shop recently and overheard the conversation behind me of a sweet woman who was having a hard day. **A really hard day.** I knew this because the words coming out of her mouth and into her cell phone were less than complimentary. God convicted me to say something, but I must admit, I was not interested. *"Lord, she does not even know me, AND she will think I'm super weird, AND she will accuse me of eavesdropping. Can't I just pray for her without actually speaking to her?"* As I battled through this imaginary conversation, my latte was served. It was **T-ime for Takeoff,** and I had a choice to make. I could simply exit and pray for her by name (after all, I knew it because she had to tell the barista!), or I could tell her that I was praying for her. **I decided to tell her.** Her eyes filled with tears as I said her name and told her that I didn't know what she was going through but God did. I'm so glad I didn't let my fears get the best of me and bank on the old adage that says, "Actions speak louder than words." Sometimes we have to **use** our words, let go of our insecurities, and **TELL** people that God loves them.

Read Isaiah 50:4 again. In addition to strengthening the weary, God wakes us up with a special alarm clock eager to hear what He has to say. This daily morning by morning discipline of getting up and sitting with the Lord is important. We can't expect the blessing until we are willing to build the relationship. We need ears to hear and hearts ready to be taught. We don't want to miss Jesus in the morning. If we do, we might miss telling about Him in coffee shops.

We can't expect the blessing until we are willing to build the relationship.

Read the following verses. What is the result of a listening ear and a teachable heart?

• **Romans 10:17**

_____

_____

_____

• **Matthew 7:24**

_____

_____

_____

• **1 Thessalonians 2:13**

_____

_____

_____

Our faith comes from hearing the Word. We are considered wise when we obey God's teaching because our faith is built on a strong foundation. Hearing and acting on the Word performs its work in us who believe. Read Isaiah 55:11 in the margin. God's Word will never come back empty. Once it is sown into our soul, it has purpose. I love that!

"So is my word that goes out from my mouth: It will not return to me empty, but will accomplish what I desire and achieve the purpose for which I sent it."

Isaiah 55:11

Read the following verses about Jesus waking up to spend time with His Captain. What were the results of His prayers?

• **Mark 1:35-39**

_____

_____

• **Luke 4:42-44**

_____

_____

I love this exercise. Jesus never slept in! He was disciplined in His T-IME for Takeoff. Notice what happened after His time of prayer. **He was eager and inspired to preach and spread the good news!** When we, too, take the time to spend our mornings with Jesus, our ears are opened to hear the Word. Our lips become a source for healing, and our hearts are open to go and preach the good news of the Kingdom of God. Amen!

God is going to teach us, inspire us, and lead us, but we have to be **still** enough to listen. We have to have teachable and eager hearts to learn. If we are going to have a one-on-one personal relationship with our Captain, the best preparation for the ride is to get to know Him. Remember, we can't expect the blessing unless we are willing to build the relationship. Wake up morning by morning, read the Word of God, and sit so you can soar into your day. Think of it like riding a bike with no hands! Ah, the freedom.

I drove by a sign last night that said, "What you look at is not necessarily what you see." Think about this for a minute. Time spent with our Master in the morning is **essential** to our takeoff preparation for the day. It's essential because our first glance at something might not be what God wants us to see. Sometimes to really see something, we have to spend T-I-M-E looking at it.

Read the following verses. Why does God want to open our eyes? What does He want us to see?

• **Psalm 119:18**

_____

_____

_____

_____   "Open my eyes to see the

_____   wonderful truths in your

                                                instructions." Psalm 119:18

• **Ephesians 1:17-19**

_____

_____

_____

_____

• **Acts 26:16-18 (Why were Paul's eyes opened and how does this affect us today?)**

_____

_____

_____

_____

• **Isaiah 42:6-8**

_____

_____

_____

_____

Why does God want to open our eyes? Because **our bike ride matters!** T-ime for Takeoff is about building a strong foundation of faith, and it begins with spending time in God's Word. We, like Paul, have a mission. We are stokers, a light for others, and servants of Christ with a message to share. God wants us to have a spirit of wisdom and revelation to know Him better so that the eyes of our hearts will be "flooded with light so we can understand the **confident hope** He has given to us" (Ephesians 1:17-19). He wants to turn our eyes from the darkness of pedaling backward which only entangles us in the chains of disappointment and regret. He wants us to pedal forward and fix our eyes on the light of His everlasting love and forgiveness. He wants us to lean into His leading and respond to His goodness. **Riding Tandem** with Jesus has the capacity to change our vision and the direction of our course. Our Captain wants to give us **hope** in a sometimes hopeless world. But the revelation of God's Word can only happen when our eyes are open, our ears are listening, our hearts are ready to receive—and our rear ends are seated.

Psalm 119:18 is a verse we will see often in **Riding Tandem.** It emphasizes that God wants to open our eyes because He wants to show us the **wonderful truths** about Him. The cool part about this verse is that the word for wonderful is *pala* meaning: marvelous, wonderful, be beyond's one power, be difficult to do.[a] This is amazing! When we take time to spend with God morning by morning, He gives us eyes to see things which only He can accomplish in our lives. We are seeing from a new perspective. His perspective. A godly perspective. Our Captain, the Sovereign Lord, has lots to teach us when we wake up morning by morning. Wipe out the sleepy seeds and **set the alarm.** No snoozing allowed!

*Lord, Thank You for this Bible study as I am learning to Ride Tandem with You. I have learned that You are the Captain of my life. You are in the front seat to steer **and** pedal. I am on the back seat where I can **only** pedal. This is so hard, Lord! I want to be in control. I want to steer my own plans. But with humility and trust, I am confident that You are leading me in the right direction. Give me eyes to see and wisdom to discern where I can stoke the fire to serve You the best. Lord, I desire a deeper connection to You, and in order to have this, I need a teachable spirit. I pray You would wake me each morning with an eager desire to listen and learn. Sometimes what I am looking at is not what You want for me to see. Give me eyes to see with a godly perspective. Sometimes life gets so upsetting that I cannot see the road ahead. Come alongside me and use Your Scripture to steer my heart. I am Yours, Lord. Use me today and teach me to lean into Your leading. Amen.*

Lesson Five/ OUR FINAL DESTINATION

Today, we are going to answer the question: Where is God leading us anyway? There is always a reason, right?

John-John and Curry were fighting about something. (As time goes on, isn't it nice to forget those little arguments you thought were going to drive you crazy?) John-John looked at me with tears forming in his eyes and said, "Mommy, Curry hit me for no reason."

Winnie, age six, who was listening from a distance, piped in with this one liner.

"Oh Mommy. (Pause for effect.) There is **always** . . . a reason."

Just typing that sentence makes me burst out laughing! After composing myself, the **truth** of her statement settled in. Yes, there is **always** a reason.

God is leading us for a reason, too. While we may not always see it, we must **remember** that we are asking God to OPEN our eyes to see the wonderful truths in His instructions.

Look up the following verses and write down where God is leading. What is our role? I'll start us off.

> **• Psalm 27:11**

> "Teach me how to live, O LORD. Lead me along the path of honesty, for my enemies are waiting for me to fall." Psalm 27:11 (NLT)

God is leading us on a straight path. The New Living Translation says that God is leading (us) along the path of honesty. Our part is to have a **teachable heart** and **follow God's leading.** Honesty is always the best policy even when it's easier to cover up the truth. This verse also reveals that there are enemies waiting for Christians to fall. Follow God's lead and you will not stumble.

Where is God leading?/ What is our Role?

• Psalm 61:1-2

_____/_____
_____/_____
_____/_____

• Psalm 23:1-4

_____/_____
_____/_____
_____/_____

• Psalm 139:23-24

_____/_____
_____/_____
_____/_____
_____/_____

• Exodus 15:13

_____/_____
_____/_____
_____/_____

God leads. Our job is to ask, to call, to cry, to remember, to search, and to try. **This is our part.** We have to do our work. We cannot expect God to wave a wand and place us on the yellow brick road. Life is certain to have its share of lions, tigers, and bears. But we have a guide, a teacher, and a loving Father who will protect us along the way. When our hearts grow faint, He is there. When we are overwhelmed, He will lead us to the rock of safety. When we are anxious, He will lead us. He is **all** we need. He renews our strength and leads us into **everlasting.**

Read Ecclesiastes 3:11. What is PLANTED in our hearts? _____

> "He has planted eternity in the human heart, but even so, people cannot see the whole scope of God's work from beginning to end." Ecclesiastes 3:11 (NLT)

Yes! **Eternity.** Last time I looked, that meant forever. Just as an acorn has the DNA to grow into a beautiful oak tree, we, too, have eternity planted in our hearts. Whether we acknowledge it or not, there is an emptiness in us that ONLY God can fill. We long for this relationship.

Whether we have been walking with God for five months, five years, or 50 years, we **all** have a longing to be closer to our Creator.

Scripture does not say that God has planted power, position, or even prosperity in our hearts. No. Our Creator, who made us His masterpiece, has planted **eternity** into our hearts. The seed of everlasting life is planted in our souls. Belief in Jesus activates the seed and inflames the passion to stoke the fire within us. Life here and now will never satisfy our deep inner longings because we were not made to live on a temporal earth. We were made to live in an eternal heaven. John 3:16 talks about this.

> "For God so loved the world that he gave his one and only Son, that whoever believes in him shall not perish but have **eternal life**."

The gift of eternity is written all over Scripture. I hope this will be a fun exercise for you as we continue to learn where God is leading us in **preparation for takeoff** each morning.

Read the following verses. What do you learn about eternal life? What personal choices lead you there?

- **John 17:1-5**

"When Jesus had spoken these words, he lifted up his eyes to heaven, and said, 'Father, the hour has come; glorify your Son that the Son may glorify you, since you have given him authority over all flesh, to give **eternal life** to all whom you have given him. And this is **eternal life**, that they **know you** the only true God, and Jesus Christ whom you have sent. I glorified you on earth, having accomplished the work that you gave me to do. And now, Father, glorify me in your own presence with the glory that I had with you before the world existed.'" John 17:1-5 (ESV)

_____
_____
_____
_____

- **John 5:24**

_____
_____
_____

- **Romans 6:22-23**

_____
_____
_____

- **Matthew 6:19-21**

"Do not store up for yourselves treasures on earth, where moths and vermin destroy, and where thieves break in and steal. But store up for yourselves treasures in heaven, where moths and vermin do not destroy, and where thieves do not break in and steal. For where your treasure is, there your heart will be also." Matthew 6:19-21

_____
_____
_____
_____
_____

LEAD ME

Eternal life is given to all who hear God's Word, believe in Jesus, and know Him as their Sovereign Lord. Confession in Christ, the Son of the Living God, saves us from death and ushers us into a life forever in the presence of a Holy God. When we ask God to be our leader, our Captain, He is leading us in lessons that not only prepare us for today, but prepare us for the ride tomorrow—and forever. **Everlasting life.** This is why our decisions for today are so important. God's leading is not just about our next steps, they are about His eternal purposes. Our opportunities for today can and will affect our tomorrow. Our choices for today have future implications. Our prayers for today have lasting effects for years to come. Are you getting this picture? God is preparing us for **eternity** while He is preparing us for **today.**

Matthew 6:19-21 calls us to store up treasures in heaven. What is the difference between an earthly treasure and a heavenly one? I am quite confident God is not talking about the American dream: How many cars we have, how big our house is, where our kids go to school, and if we have a latte machine. I love the bumper sticker that reads: "You can't take a U-Haul to heaven!" God treasures open hearts and open hands. When we follow Him to serve the poor, help those in need, give up worry, smile with thankful hearts, obey His teachings, live with humility, love unconditionally, hope expectantly, and believe confidently . . . we are storing up treasures in heaven! James tells us that one of the treasures is patiently enduring testing and temptations (James 1:12). If we are leaning into the leading of God and allowing Him to steer our tandem bike into everlasting life, then we are storing up treasures in heaven.

Eternity is our final destination.

Great job this week! In closing, write a prayer to your Captain. Tell Him what you would like to learn from Riding Tandem as you ride into eternity together. Try not to clutch on to the handlebars too tightly. Let go and learn to lean into His leading.

_____

_____

_____

_____

_____

_____

_____

_____

_____

_____

_____

_____

_____

_____

_____

_____

_____

_____

This week, we learned the basics of Riding Tandem. We learned to take the lead from the Captain and lean into His leading each day. **T-ime for Takeoff** is about taking the T-I-M-E to get to **know** our Captain, surrendering the front seat, and trusting Him.

We will learn THREE things about our Captain today.

1. God will _____ us for every good work.
2. We are His good work created in _____ _____ for good works.
3. When He begins a good work, He _____ a good work.

Riding Tandem is not about a religion. It's about a _____.

1. God will EQUIP us for every good work.

• Our works are directly connected to our _____.
• To identify our work, we have to identify our _____.

> "All Scripture is God-breathed and is useful for teaching, rebuking, correcting and training in righteousness, so that the servant of God may be thoroughly equipped for every good work."
>
> 2 Timothy 3:16-17

2. We are His good work created in Christ for good works.

• To prepare means: to make ready, to make beforehand in mind and _____.

3. When God creates a good work, He will complete the good work.

• To carry on means: to accomplish, to finish, to execute, to complete
• Christ will _____ us.

Answers: equip, Christ Jesus, finishes, relationship, gifts, passions, purpose, fellowship, complete

Week TWO: Lesson One/ ALIGNMENT

Before we begin week two, let's take time to review.

T-ime for Takeoff prepares us to ride with God in this tandem adventure called life. God is our Captain who steers, pedals, and leads our days. We are the co-captains and stokers that pedal to receive the power. The tandem bike was built for two just like our relationship with God. We have to know our Captain personally to believe with confidence and trust in His leading. Spending time with Him morning by morning opens our eyes to see and ears to hear His wonderful truths. God leads us along straight paths and ultimately into eternity. What a week. There is so much more to learn!

Riding Tandem uses the acronym T • A • N • D • E • M to mark the chapters for our week's lessons. This week, we come to the letter "A" which represents **A-lignment.** A-lignment is essential when riding tandem. Why? When we are not A-ligned, we will fall off the bike. Plain and simple. In bicycle terms, this action is called **tandem toppling** (for real!). The Captain has to steady the bike before the co-captain can hop on. When there is no Captain to balance the bike, the rear rider will topple.

What great imagery! We, too, will fall when we do not allow our Captain to steady our lives. He is always ready. When we can barely open our eyes, God is waiting for us to wake up so He can steady the bike for our journey ahead. Look at the synonyms for the word **steady.** Which one listed below best describes God to you? Circle your answer.

Steady: immovable, never failing, solid as a rock, steadfast, durable, constant, reliable, safe, unchangeable.

I liked the word **durable.** It makes me think of the Duracell® battery. They last the longest and have extra-staying power. Duracell® promises that "their batteries will hold out the longest, by supplying power long after their competitor's batteries have died out."[1]

God, like Duracell®, has durability.

What does Deuteronomy 31:6 say about God's staying power?

_____
_____

> "Be strong and courageous. Do not be afraid or terrified because of them, for the LORD your God goes with you; he will never leave you nor forsake you."
>
> Deuteronomy 31:6

God is always reliable, and He promises never to leave us, especially when we are afraid. He is our Captain and will steady the bike for us, every day, before we hit the day running (or biking).

Read the following verses. Why do you think God's durable qualities help us avoid tandem toppling? I know this is a big list, but God is a big God. We need to remind ourselves how powerful and durable He is to steady our lives. Forge ahead!

• **Psalm 111:7**

_____
_____

- **Hebrews 6:17**

"God also bound himself with an oath, so that those who received the promise could be perfectly sure that he would never change his mind." Hebrews 6:17 (NLT)

_____

_____

- **Hebrews 13:8**

_____

_____

- **1 John 1:5**

_____

_____

- **John 14:6**

_____

_____

- **John 1:1**

"In the beginning was the Word, and the Word was with God, and the Word was God." John 1:1

_____

_____

- **Matthew 5:48**

_____

_____

God is not only durable, He is also faithful and trustworthy. **God is unchangeable.** He is the same yesterday, today, and tomorrow. He is the way, the truth, the life, and in Him there is no darkness at all. He has been here all along and is **perfect.** Oh boy! That's enough credentials for me!

Here's the deal: I am not really worried about God's durability, but I am concerned about mine. I am not always trustworthy (forgot to pick up Winnie from ballet last night!). I don't have all the right answers (although I like to think I do). It's not easy for me to climb on the back seat when I like to know where I am going. I like being in charge and in control. I will even confess that sometimes I doubt God's direction. When it comes to **A-lignment**, I need to be first in line.

In 6th grade, I broke my right arm chasing boys up a tree. I know. I know. Hindsight is foresight. My eyes were looking up at the boys and not on the limb that was too unstable to hold me. I came crashing down. All nine feet. I braced the fall with my right arm and crack . . . no more alignment. I remember to this day the pain of the novocaine shot injected into my wrist before it was put back into A-lignment. Ouch.

The same is true when we are out of A-lignment with our Captain. **Our life hurts.** Sometimes it's easy to see, but often it's more subtle than a bone out of place. We might have a sense something is out of balance, but it's hard to detect. We need **new eyes** to see from His perspective. Open our eyes, Lord, that we may see the wonderful things.

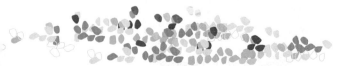

Read Sarah Young's quote from Jesus Calling on February 10th.[2]

> "As you align yourself with my perspective, you can sort out what is important and what is not. Don't fall into the trap of being constantly on the go. Many many things people do in my name have no value in My kingdom. To avoid meaningless work, stay in continual communication with me."

To A-lign means to change (something) so that it agrees with or matches something else.[3] When we are in A-lignment with God, we agree that Jesus is our Captain and will ride where He takes us. Our lives have been changed so that our spirit matches His leading. We are in sync. We are pedaling together. We are **Riding Tandem.**

As we see in the quote from Sarah Young, my honest confession of chasing boys up a tree, and the advertisement for Duracell®, there is **competition for our power source.** I like to call them Kingdom competitors. These are traps that supply false power and have no value in God's Kingdom. What do you think they are? Volunteering too much? Busyness? Stress? Over commitments? Keeping up with the Joneses?

What are the obvious and subtle things in your life that keep you out of A-lignment and compete with God for your attention? Take some time and ask God to show you areas in your life that you might need to change.

_____
_____
_____
_____
_____
_____

What is competing for our attention according to the following verses? What should our response be to allow God to steady our lives?

Our Competition/ Our Response

• **John 12:43-46**

_____/_____
_____/_____
_____/_____

• **Psalm 32:3-5**

_____/_____
_____/_____
_____/_____
_____/_____

• **Ephesians 4:29**

_____/_____
_____/_____
_____/_____

• **Ephesians 4:31-5:2**

_____/_____
_____/_____
_____/_____
_____/_____

Kingdom competitors desire mans' approval over God's approval. (This is biblical slang for people pleasing.) Keeping our sins a secret will eat away at our physical and emotional health. Gossip never builds up our friendships. Unwholesome talk always tears people down and reveals our judgmental hearts. Anger, bitterness, and rage destroy our A-lignment with God. Trusting in the things of this world for our balance will leave us miserable and empty. If we desire to be in continual communication with God, He **promises** to steady the bike for us. It's our choice. Every time we choose to hold our tongue, we choose to hop on the back and let God steer our circumstance. Every time we refrain from anger and rage, we choose to give God the control of our emotional state. Kingdom competitors are **false power sources.** They distract us from following God's lead and leave us at the bottom of a tree with a broken branch and a broken arm. We are out of A-lignment and our souls hurt.

Ephesians 5:1-2 gives us a solution for tandem toppling. It's living a life of love, imitating Christ, and being a fragrant aroma. Girls, we aren't smellin' so good when we seek praise from men, walk in secrecy, gossip, and stress about how overwhelmed and overcommitted we are. This is FALSE POWER and leads to insecurity and out of A-lignment living. 1 John 1:5 says that God is light. He is the true light source with lasting staying power. He is steadying the bike for us each day. He is our DURACELL®. We need to be A-ligned with Him and only Him to avoid **tandem toppling.**

"Follow God's example, therefore, as dearly loved children and walk in the way of love, just as Christ loved us and gave himself up for us as a fragrant offering and sacrifice to God."

Ephesians 5:1-2

Lord, thank You that You are waiting to steady me each and everyday. You are the only power source I need. Help me when I get unbalanced and want to be in the control seat. Please convict me when I am swayed to gossip, anger, people pleasing, and discontent. You are so faithful. You are the truth. Teach me to believe and trust that Your leading is perfect. You see the road ahead and will lead me in the right direction. I love You, Jesus. You are unchanging. You are the perfect Captain. Help me not to tandem topple! Amen.

Lesson Two RIDING PAST THE GATE

As a graphic designer, I love the A-lignment tool.

Why? Because when you are typing a document, one simple button will **justify** your work—instantly. Left justify, right justify, or center. One click and shazam! Your work is aligned. It's a beautiful tool. The Bible tells us that once we confess Jesus, we are made **right with God.** It's like hitting the "shazam" key. Jesus' justification tool was His blood shed on the cross for our unjustified state. Read the following verses and learn how we are made right with God when we believe in His one and only Son. It's so very awesome.

What do the following verses teach us about justification? How are we made right with God?

• **Romans 3:22-24**

"We are made **right** in God's sight when we **trust in Jesus Christ to take away our sins.** And we all can be saved in this same way, no matter who we are or what we have done. For all have sinned; all fall short of God's glorious standard. Yet now God in his gracious kindness declares us not guilty. He has done this through Christ Jesus, who has freed us by taking away our sins. Our belief in Jesus Christ **aligns us** with God. It makes us **right with Him.**" (NLT)

LEAD ME

• **Romans 10:9-11**

_____

_____

_____

_____

_____

_____

• **Romans 5:1, 8-11**

_____

_____

_____

_____

_____

_____

• **2 Corinthians 5:17-21**

_____

_____

_____

_____

_____

_____

This is a lot to digest! I think we all need to slowly read these verses again. **Our belief in Jesus Christ A-ligns us with God.** We are made **right** with Him when we confess with our lips that He is Lord and trust that His life, death, and resurrection have the power to take away our sin. We have **all** fallen short of His glory. Therefore, no other power source will do. Jesus is the **only** power source we need. Our personal response to **who Jesus is** changes the direction of our course and destines us for eternity. When we choose Jesus, we are choosing to be made right with God, to align ourselves to His leading, and to agree to our position on the back seat. But this is not the end!

The choice to believe in Christ is where the journey **begins!** Yes, we are saved from sin and have the guarantee of eternal life, but this is not all there is. We are saved to live out an abundant life for Christ—right here on earth.

What does Philippians 2:12b-13 say about living a life for Christ? Who is working in us?

_____

_____

_____

"God **is** working in you, giving you the power and desire to do what pleases Him."

Philippians 2:13 (NLT)

Yes! **God** Himself, the Almighty Captain, IS working IN us. Notice the present tense. God **is** currently active in our lives through the person of the Holy Spirit. After Jesus ascended into heaven, the Holy Spirit came in full force to take His place—not in bodily form, but in spirit. He came to empower us, guide us, teach us, lead us, and plant in us God's desire to share the gospel and do His will. When we understand that the full power of Jesus is living **in us,** we will understand that life is to be lived to the fullest in this present moment!

This is where **Riding Tandem** gets exciting! When we believe in Christ, HE LIVES IN US. Our faith is not stagnant, but rather a **continuing** process where God **is** working in us giving us His desires and power to do His will. But, we must be warned, as tandem riders, we still need to be on the lookout for Kingdom competitors.

What does John 10:9-10 say about living an abundant life. Who wants to steal it?

_____

_____

_____

_____

_____

Jesus is the gate. When we enter the gate, we are saved. We are aligned with God and made right in His sight. But believing in Christ does not stop at the gate. This is not a signed, sealed, and delivered kind of story. Once we enter a life with Christ, we enter a joy-filled life riding tandem with the King of Kings. We know our Captain. We love Him. We have 100% confidence that He is taking us in the right direction. But there is an enemy who wants to steal our one-on-one relationship with Christ. Satan is a deceiver and wants us to believe that even though we have accepted Christ, we don't really need Him every day. We compartmentalize our Christianity for Sundays, Sunday School, and Bible study. For the most part, we think we are just fine pedaling on our own. We enjoy being in the front seat. We say our prayers at night and even have a Christian fish on the back of our swaggin' wagon. But something is missing. We are empty inside and feel defeated and useless. Jesus becomes just a religion, a tradition, and our faith seems artificial. Do you ever feel this way? Sister, I am here to tell you **there is hope!** Jesus did not save you to leave you sitting at the gate waiting for eternal life. No! He saved you to live an ABUNDANT life here and now. He saved you so that you could have freedom and protection in His pasture. He saved you so you could ride—hands free—tandem with Him. Read the words of Major W. Ian Thomas from his book: *The Saving Life of Christ.*

> "How stupid would it be to buy a car with a powerful engine under the hood and then to spend your days pushing it! Thwarted and exhausted, you would wish to discard it as a useless thing. Yet, to some of you who are Christians, this may be God's word to your heart. When God redeemed you through the precious blood of His dear Son, He placed a powerful engine under the hood —nothing less than the resurrection life of God the Son, made over to you in the person of God, the Holy Spirit. Stop pushing! Step in and switch on and expose every hill of circumstance, of opportunity, of temptation, of perplexity—no matter how threatening—to the divine energy that is available." Major W. Ian Thomas[4]

Because of Christ's sacrifice for us, God hit the justification button the moment we confessed Jesus is the Christ, the Son of the Living God. Everyday we have the opportunity to have Christ LIVE in us. Not just on Sundays. Not just in hospital rooms. Not just for saying our prayers at night. Jesus has placed a powerful engine called the Holy Spirit into our hearts. Stop pushing and trying to live this life on your own power. Don't let the enemy steal your joy. Jesus is ready to live through you and is completely adequate to fill your every need. We need to get into **A-lignment** with Him and trust Him to steady the tandem. No tandem toppling for this girl. I need Him to A-lign me today. How about you?

Dear Father, help me to live this abundant life— for You are living inside of me. Today, I give You my concerns, my worries, and my fears. I know You will steady my life and steer me in Your direction because You are working inside of me giving me the power and desire to do Your will. You came not for me just to sit at the gate, but to enjoy an abundant life in the protection of Your pasture. A-lign me with Your Spirit as I Ride Tandem with You. No hands. Amen.

Lesson Three/ PRAYERFUL, WATCHFUL, THANKFUL

Yesterday, we learned that our confession of Jesus makes us in perfect A-lignment with Him. But that's not where our faith ends!

God placed His power IN us to act according to His will. His desire is for us to walk in our faith everyday, shining the light of Jesus for all to see. Today, we will look at what it takes to **stay in A-lignment**, day-to-day, as we ride tandem with the Lord.

> **Please look up Colossians 4:2, write down the verse, and highlight the three words that will keep us A-ligned with God.**
>
> _____
> _____
> _____

The three actions that keep us aligned with God are:

1. Being prayerful
2. Being watchful
3. Being thankful

Let's begin with being prayerful—**devoted in prayer.** The word for devotion means: to adhere to, to be steadfast, attentive to, to persevere in a place.[5]

Praying with devotion is being **committed** to something.
Praying with devotion is being unwilling to move, to be **steadfast.**
Praying with devotion is **to press in** on . . . even when it's hard.
Praying with devotion is **A-ligning** yourself with a godly perspective.

I love that the root word for devotion is to have **strength**. The idea of being devoted in prayer describes someone with durable power.

> **Who do you know with a durable prayer life? What stands out to you in this person's character?**
>
> _____
> _____
> _____
> _____
> _____

The next action that keeps us aligned with God is being **watchful.**

Watchful means: to give strict attention to, to be cautious, to be awake.[6] The word watchful is used many times in the Old Testament to describe men who were watching out for the enemy. Watch guards were usually stationed on high walls where they could get a better perspective to see the enemy approaching. These men were awake and always on the lookout for Kingdom competitors. They remained attentive at **all** times. When we combine devoting ourselves to prayer with being watchful, we, too, will see from a new perspective—a godly perspective. This higher level allows us to be on the lookout for the enemy who tries to deceive us with false power. Devotion to prayer and being watchful **A-ligns us with God's perspective** so we can see the things God is doing in our life.

Thankfulness is the third element in this verse. This is the anchor action for staying in sync with God. Why? Because life is hard and circumstances can be heartbreaking. Sometimes it takes divine "Duracell® power" to **see** the lasting things for which God wants us to be thankful, especially when our prayers don't turn out the way we expect. Remember, the word for wonderful in Psalm 119:18? Wonderful means to see the things that are impossible for us to handle on our own. We can't do it by ourselves. This is why we need our Captain's strength and perspective to keep us from tandem toppling. He's got the power and authority. When we give it **all** to Him with thankful hearts and lean on Him when life is not easy, **we stay in A-lignment.** Prayerful. Watchful. Thankful.

My oldest sister was diagnosed with a brain tumor in 2003. She noticed she could not hear on the phone and went in for testing. Days later, she discovered there was a tumor behind her right ear that had wrapped around her facial nerve. Before my brother-in-law told her the diagnosis, he prayed for her and **thanked God.**

Hard? Yes. Impossible? Not with God.

After two surgeries and the complete removal of her ear drum, she is tumor free. She will be the first to tell you that having a thankful heart is what got her through this difficult time. My sister's devotion in prayer gave her supernatural strength to press on and trust in Jesus. She had eyes to see with a new perspective because the Holy Spirit was under her hood. She woke up in the mornings to have devoted prayer time and kept watch for her Captain. As a result, she maintained a thankful heart that kept her aligned with Christ and her spirit tuned into His leading. The situation was not easy by any means, and God did not choose to take her pain away. But He never left her side as He balanced the tandem for her each day to hop on with new conviction that He was in charge. Do you see the strength that is given when we press on and stay in A-lignment? He gives us the power to keep pedaling! My sister doesn't just know about Jesus. She believes IN Jesus. There is a big difference. When we believe IN Jesus, our hearts will not be troubled and worry is replaced with **peace.** That's true A-lignment.

"Let not your hearts be troubled. Believe **IN** God; believe also **IN** me." John 14:1

How's your A-lignment today? What are you experiencing in your life right now where you need to draw on God's strength and perspective?

_____
_____
_____
_____

Look up the following verses. What actions are needed in order to press on through difficult situations? Where can you see devotion to prayer, being watchful, and being thankful as key elements to each verse?

- **Philippians 3:12-14**

_____
_____

- **Hebrews 6:1-2**

"So come on, let's leave the preschool finger painting exercises on Christ and get on with the grand work of art. Grow up in Christ. The basic foundational truths are in place: turning your back on "salvation by self-help" and turning in trust toward God; . . . Let's get on with it!" Hebrew 6:1-3 (MSG)

_____
_____
_____
_____

• James 1:2-4

_____

_____

_____

_____

The Message translation speaks to my creative heart! Let's leave finger painting behind and grow up. Staying in alignment is trusting IN your foundation of belief. It is not by surprise that James tells us that hard times build our faith. Our **testimonies** are the stories of our faith. Yes, they are tests—tests that God wants us to pass with His divine strength. But it takes daily prayer, watchful eyes, and thankful hearts. There is freedom in the pasture and freedom to look forward, forgetting what is behind. We do not have to be afraid, worry, or pedal harder. However, the enemy loves to keep our focus on past mistakes, poor choices, and big time mess-ups. Paul tells us to keep our eyes open, focus on Jesus, and press on towards the prize which Christ calls us heavenward. Again, **our destination is eternity**, but **our goal is to know Jesus in the present moment.**

Our kitten, Turbo, was found under the hood of our babysitter's car. We named him Turbo because not only was he meowing under the engine, but also because this little guy was fast! Maybe too fast. One night, while irritating our golden doodle, Phineas, Turbo's speed got the best of him. He tripped over Phinney's paw going ninety to nothing and fractured his leg. Of course, Phinney never fessed up to the crime, but Turbo was out of power. He was out of alignment.

The next day, Turbo was still trying to move as fast as he could, but his leg was keeping him from mach speed. I have to tell you that it was quite comical watching this little feline attack life as super kitten, while trying to convince himself that nothing was wrong. The $200 X-rays, however, were not as comical. The fracture was confirmed.

Why am I telling you this story? Just as we are called to ride tandem with Jesus, I believe Jesus uses the stories of our lives to "tandem" with what He is teaching us! Through Turbo, Jesus taught me that if I want to be A-ligned with God's perspective and have eyes to see His wonderful truth, I have to slow down. Slow down to **pray**. Slow down and be **watchful** for the enemy who is trying to trip me up. Slow down to be **thankful** for little surprises under the hood! When we are out of A-lignment, going ninety to nothing, we are too busy to pray, too unfocused to be watchful, and too self-centered to be thankful. As we discussed in week one, T-ime for Takeoff, the time we spend with our Lord is critical to how we will approach our day. If we live life like super kitty, sooner or later we are going to trip. Oh, we can try to fake our fracture (and we do a pretty good job of it), but just like Turbo, the results are in. We are broken. When I am not in A-lignment with my Captain, my thoughts, emotions, feelings, desires, wants, passions, and dreams are usually about what Annie wants. When I choose to A-lign myself with God's perspective, my thoughts, emotions, feelings, desires, wants, passions and dreams match those He wants for me. Big difference. Thank goodness God doesn't need X-rays to look into our hearts. He knows our motives, and He can see our intentions. We might try to fool everyone else, but in the end, we are just fools. **Turbo Fools.**

Look up Proverbs 28:26. What is the difference between someone who tries to pedal on her own and the one who rides tandem with God as her Captain?

_____

_____

_____

_____

_____

_____

_____

_____

My NIV footnotes tell me that to walk in wisdom is the same as trusting in God.[7] In context with our James passage we read earlier, James 1:5-6 tells us that if we lack wisdom (and who doesn't?) we need to ASK God who gives generously without finding fault. We are only fools to think we can pedal and steer our own lives in our own power. James also tells us we need to BELIEVE and not doubt. Doubt is another cheap shot from the enemy. God's Word is the truth, and it never changes. Ask for His wisdom and trust in His leading. When you are having a turbo-kind-of-day, **pray** with devotion. **Watch** with your eyes open. And give **thanks** in ALL circumstances.

Read 2 Thessalonians 2:16-17 as our closing prayer.

"May our Lord Jesus Christ himself and God our Father, who loved us and by his grace give us **eternal encouragement** and good hope, encourage your hearts and **strengthen you** in every good deed and word." Amen.

> "If any of you lacks wisdom, you should ask God, who gives generously to all without finding fault, and it will be given to you. 6 But when you ask, you must believe and not doubt, because the one who doubts is like a wave of the sea, blown and tossed by the wind."
>
> James 1:5-6

Lesson Four/ BAND-AID OR BOLD?

Today we are going to study a biblical character who graduates from Christian Kindergarten and ends up with her Masters in Divinity—Queen Esther.

To give you a brief update, Esther is the Queen of Persia and the wife to King Xerxes. Mordecai is a Jew and also Esther's cousin who raised her after her parents died. The story unfolds as Mordecai finds out that an evil man named Haman has set a decree to "destroy, kill, and annihilate all the Jews—young and old, women and little children—on a single day, the thirteenth day of the twelfth month . . ." (Esther 3:13). Mordecai is found at the city gates in sack cloth, wailing and crying when Esther learns about the situation.

Please read Esther 4:1-17. (It's long but worth it!)

   What is Esther's first response when she learns about Mordecai's distress? (Esther 4:4-5)

   _____

   _____

   _____

   What is Esther's first reaction when she learns of the decree and what Mordecai wants her to do? (Esther 4:10-11)

   _____

   _____

   _____

   What is Mordecai's response to her initial complaint? (Esther 4:12-14)

   _____

   _____

   _____

How did Esther graduate from kindergarten and move with power and perseverance to get her Master's degree? (Esther 4:15-5:1)

_____

_____

_____

_____

When Queen Esther learns of the decree to annihilate the Jews, (an edict which could not be reversed because of the king's signature approval), we see her frightened and afraid. Her response to Mordecai was something like this: "You want me to do what? You DO know that I will be killed instantly if I walk in front of the king unannounced, don't you? He hasn't called for me in three weeks and . . . Mordecai, are you crazy? **Seriously?**" I doubt the conversation went like that, but you get the picture!

On a side note, when your house gets super crazy like mine, does everyone's name become—**"Seriously?"**

• "Mom, I forgot to tell you that I have a science project due tomorrow. The good news is that I am making cupcakes with icing from different kinds of butter." **Seriously?**

• "Mom, I know you just had the rugs cleaned, but Phineas (our golden doodle) just had an accident on the stairwell carpet." **Seriously?**

• "Mom, I left my soccer socks at home, and I know you don't do anything while we are at school, so can you bring them to me by 3:00?" **Seriously?**

• "Honey, I have a client that needs to be taken to dinner, and I would L-O-V-E for you to go with us. Can you get dressed and meet us in fifteen minutes?" **Seriously?**

• Esther, I know the king hasn't seen you in a while (Uh, why not by the way?) but your own life is in just as much danger as ours. You DO remember that you are a Jew, right? So, put on your Big Girl Pants and go ask the king to spare the Jews from being destroyed—now." **SERIOUSLY?**

Mordecai sends her this response—one that dog ears the pages of many Bibles, including mine.

"Do not think that because you are in the king's house you alone of all the Jews will escape. For if you remain silent at this time, relief and deliverance for the Jews will **arise from another place,** but you and your father's family will perish. And who knows but that you have come to royal position for such a time as this?" Esther 4:13-14

Esther was at a crossroads with a serious decision to make. If we reflect back to week one, day three, Esther had the same decision the disciples had when Jesus asked them, "Who do **you** say that I am?" Who was God to Esther? Was He just a myth? Was He just a childhood fairy tale that Mordecai had taught her day in and day out? Were the stories of Abraham, Isaac, and Jacob really true? Could God be trusted in a time like this? Was she going to take control and steer this journey? Or was she going to trust God, believe in the miracles of the past, and get on the back of the tandem and pedal? I can't help but to think that perhaps Mordecai was praying: "Train up a child in the way he should go, and when he is old he will not depart from it" (Proverbs 22:6).

This is a great question for all of us. What does our faith look like when we cannot see the road ahead, decisions need to be made, action needs to be taken, life is hectic, and the journey is scary? Do we choose to put our own agendas and selfish ambitions first? Or do we walk in wisdom, trusting that God is faithful?

• Do we have a **BAND-AID faith**—a quick solution that covers up the pain so we can pretend it's not there? Or is our faith **BOLD**—willing to surrender our agendas, our comfort, and trust God with the impossible?

• Do we have an **APATHETIC faith**—hoping with time the problem will just disappear?
Or is our faith **AUTHENTIC** —recognizing the problem, our weakness, and CALL on God to empower us so we can A-lign ourselves with His perspective?

Read Esther 4:15-17 and write down where you can see her A-lignment happening. Keep in mind: devotion to prayer, being watchful, and thankful.

_____
_____
_____
_____
_____
_____
_____

I love that Esther does not let kingdom competitors influence her actions. She does not ask Mordecai for advice. She doesn't ask her friends for advice. She doesn't text her latest drama or post on social media. She decides to align herself with the movement of her circumstance, praying, watching, and trusting that her Captain will lead her in the right direction. She is pedaling for her life. We see Esther go through a complete character change from a scared little queen to an **empowered daughter of the King.** We see her graduate from:

- Devastated to DEVOTED
- Problematic to PRAYERFUL
- Worried to WATCHFUL
- Terrified to THANKFUL

Esther gathers her maids together and asks Mordecai to gather ALL the Jews who are in Susa to PRAY and FAST for her—to not eat or drink for three days or nights. She makes the BOLD decision that when the time of fasting is over, she will approach the king unannounced even if it's against the law and her life is on the line.

Circling back to the question on page 32, what does your faith look like when you cannot see the road ahead? Do you post on social media or call on your friends to pray for you? What is going on in your life right now that prompts you to take off the band-aid and move to bolder faith? What have you learned in Riding Tandem that can empower your faith from apathetic to authentic?

_____
_____
_____
_____
_____
_____
_____
_____
_____
_____

We will never know what transformed Esther's life in those three days of concentrated prayer and fasting, but I have a few ideas! One BIG truth we can take home today is this: **Riding Tandem** with God changes us. When we depend upon the power of the King, our life is different. We see life from a different perspective—His Kingdom perspective. Let's leave with this question and ponder the answers.

Lead Me

What would our lives look like if we truly believed that Jesus LIVES inside of us?

Major Thomas tells us that the content of the gospel is not just heaven *one day,* but Christ *right now.* To preach anything less than this is what he describes as "evan-jellyfish—folk with no spiritual vertebrae."

> "A living body breathes, and a living faith breathes with divine action. A living faith breathes with the activity of Jesus Christ. It is your LIVING Faith in the adequacy of the One who is IN YOU, which releases His divine action through you."[8]

A-lignment with Jesus is taking our every minute thoughts, choices, beliefs, concerns, hopes, and fears and filtering it with the truth of God's Word knowing and BELIEVING that Christ is IN you. A-lignment is —

> "exposing by faith every situation as it arises, to the all-suffienciency of the One who indwells you by His life. Can ANY situation arise, in any circumstance, for which He is not adequate? Any pressure, promise, problem, responsibility, or temptation for which the Lord Jesus Himself is not adequate?"[9]

Great question.

Esther thought so. Tomorrow we will find out how GOD released His divine power through her as she surrendered to hop on the back, pedal, and let God steer. I can feel the breeze already.

Lord, thank You for the example of Queen Esther. I am so glad we can relate to a woman in the Bible who went through some "seriously" moments. I am also thankful that someone else gets scared to step into the unknown. Thank You for teaching me that through being watchful, prayerful, and thankful, I can change my faith from apathetic to authentic. Keep me in line with Your teachings so I can step out in faith with Your power in me. Today I choose to lean into Your leading and Ride Tandem with You. Amen.

Lesson Five POWER TO PEDAL

Yesterday I was on a plane that took off on a very short runway.

(No, I was not sitting in the emergency aisle. I have been permanently banned from that seat.) Before we took off, we parked at the end of the tarmac where the airplane revved the engines. When the pilot released the brakes, we catapulted down the runway like a rocket being released from a slingshot. We needed Duracell® power for a short distance.

Esther did, too.

She needed divine power to catapult her into God's will.

For three days, Esther prepared her heart for divine strength to take action and stand up for the Jewish nation. Again, the Bible does not record what Esther learned during those three days, but I believe God **revealed** Himself to her in three ways:

1. God revealed Himself to her personally.
2. God revealed His plan for her to pursue.
3. God revealed her past so she could have power to pedal into her future.

The word reveal means: to uncover, to bring to light, to make plain, to lay open what has been covered up. We see reveal in the word **Revelation**—apokalypto: the revealing, the uncovering of the ultimate victory of good and evil.[10]

1. God revealed Himself to her personally.

Our relationship with God is a **personal** one. Our tandem journey is built for two. Esther had grown up in the Jewish faith just as many of us have grown up in a "Christian" home, but there comes a point in **all** of our lives when we have to decide who Jesus is . . . to us. Not our friends. Not our parents. But, to us—personally. This was Esther's moment. God was holding out His hand and steadying the bike for the Queen. He does the same for us.

Look up the following verses and write down how God reveals Himself to us on a personal level. What are His actions, and what are our responses? 🚲

GOD's Action/ OUR Response

• **Isaiah 40:10-11**

_____/_____
_____/_____
_____/_____

• **Isaiah 41:10**

_____/_____
_____/_____
_____/_____

• **Exodus 14:13-14**

_____/_____
_____/_____
_____/_____

Isaiah 40:10 addresses God with two names. In the King James Version it reads: "Behold, the **Lord God** will come with might." Lord (with a capital L) is *Adonay* in Hebrew and is always used to describe God. This word is used when God is submissively and reverently addressed and also spoken in place of Yahweh in a Jewish display of reverence.[11] Next we see the word God used: *Yĕhovah*. This means the "existing One" and is the proper name of the One true God.[12] Here we see, side by side, two names for our powerful God. I believe Adonay Yehovah whispered into the stillness of Esther's heart that **He was enough**. He would take her right hand, steady her fears, and strengthen her with His divine "Duracell®" power. Isaiah 40:11 shows us our Captain's tenderness on a personal level. He is described as a Shepherd who gathers His sweet lambs into His arms, carries them close to His heart, and LEADS them. Gathers. Carries. **Leads.** Let those words sink into your soul.

2. God revealed His plan for her to pursue.

God reveals His plans when we are still enough to pray, watch, and have thankful hearts to obediently step into His plan. Three days of fasting with God empowered Esther to step with boldness into a powerless situation. Why do I say this? Esther had no authority—even as the Queen going before her husband unannounced. This proves a good point. In God's economy, we don't need the world's positioning. We only need God's **power.**

Again, the verse: "Open my eyes that I may SEE the WONDERFUL things in your law"(Psalm 119:18), means open my eyes to the plans You have for me that are beyond my strength to accomplish on my own.[13] Can you believe the word for open means: to reveal, to uncover, to make known? As she sat in the presence of the Lord opening her eyes to **see,** He was **uncovering** His plan for her. Esther was filling up with holy jet fuel to propel her with amazing power before the King . . . in the power of THE KING.

Imagine if Esther was impulsive and went before the king to declare her cause **before** three days of prayer and fasting. Hmmm. I think we might have a different ending! When we have decisions to make, it is critical to sit before the King of Kings and ask Him to reveal His plan for us to pursue. Don't be impulsive and pedal in your own strength. Take note of Esther's position of prayer, open your eyes, fast, ask your friends for prayer, and sit in the stillness of the Lord. Here's a truth to ride on:

> If God is revealing something to you, He wants to DO something through you.

"The LORD gives strength to his people; the LORD blesses his people with peace."

Psalm 29:11

Read Psalm 29:11. With what does God want to fill us?

_____

Yes. **PEACE.** Peace is always a component of God's power to step into a decision. If you don't have peace, **don't move.** Keep praying, be watchful, and always have a thankful heart.

3. God revealed her past so she could have the power to pedal into her future.

It's always a good exercise to REMEMBER the faithfulness of the Lord, especially when making a big decision. That's why keeping a journal is a great idea. Personal journals help us look back and SEE where God has led us— even when we were scared and unsure. Angry. Discouraged. Confused. We can read and remember where God held our hand, steadied our bike, and did not let us tandem topple. I am not saying the outcome was always what we desired. But, if we are believers in Jesus, we can rest in the promise of knowing that God's plans for us are **good** (Jeremiah 29:11).

What do you think God revealed to Esther about her past that led her to step boldly before the King? Did He remind her of the stories Mordecai had placed in her heart as a child about the promise given to Abraham (Genesis 13:14-17)? Did He remind her of His choice to place her in the palace "for such a time as this" so she could be the vehicle of God's mercy to the Jews to save the nation? If we happen to discover Esther's ancient journal, what would be written inside? In my Bible study for tween girls called BRAVE, I challenged them to make an Esther journal. I gave them four questions to consider when making a big decision.

- First column: What decision do you need to make in this situation?
- Second column: If you were in control, what actions would you take?
- Third column: Because God is in control, how are you going to obey His leading?
- Fourth column: Write down God's faithfulness in this situation.

Grab a blank journal and make your columns. This is a great exercise and one I highly recommend. (I have designed a sample at the end of this chapter!) When we are in tune with God through devotion in prayer, being watchful, and giving thanks, we are in A-lignment and **Riding Tandem** with Him. God will reveal Himself to us personally, He will reveal His plans for us to pursue, and He will reveal our past so we can pedal into our future.

To end our week in A-lignment, I want to review the story of Esther. We can see clearly that she devoted herself in prayer and had watchful eyes to see God's plan and take action. But, where is the thanksgiving? Sit back and watch. God is so amazing!

If you continue reading, you will find that Esther was successful in approaching the King. Haman was killed, and the Jews were saved. Every year, even to the present day, the Jews celebrate **Purim**—the day the Jews were delivered from the hand of Haman. Purim is a special feast that celebrates God's goodness and provision.

Read Esther 9:18-22. How did the Jews celebrate and give thanks to God?

_____

_____

_____

What a day of thanksgiving!

As I am writing today's lesson for **Riding Tandem**, I am also thinking about Thanksgiving. (It's tomorrow!) Thanksgiving is a day of joy and feasting. We have so much to be thankful for.

My original cover for Riding Tandem was a painting of Winnie, my 13-year-old, on a tandem bike at the beach. I painted the first seat empty with her riding on the back casting two shadows onto the sand. Because it was spring break and H-O-T, she was my only willing model. With mosquitoes at an all-time high, my other children ditched me for air-conditioning. I don't blame them.

As I was painting, I wondered, *"Lord, this is a women's Bible study, and not a little girl's study. Why would I paint this?"* He sweetly leaned in, steadied the bike for me, and whispered this truth.

"Annie, truly I tell you, unless you change and become like children,
you will never enter the Kingdom of God." Matthew 18:13

Ah, yes. This makes sense now. God not only wants us to get on the back, He also wants for us to come to Him like a child, with unwavering **trust**, like Esther. My friend told me a story recently about how her grandchildren trust her when she picks them up from school. She said, "Annie, they just hop right in the backseat. They never ask me where we are going. They never ask me what we are going to do. They simply hop into the car and TRUST. **It's a beautiful thing."**

Yes, it is.

It's a beautiful thing when we:

- Learn to stay in **A-lignment** with the King of Kings by leaning in and trusting His lead.

- Have a day-to-day **relationship** with our Captain.

- Humble ourselves to **surrender** our agenda and trust in His perfect plan.

- **Believe** even though it's hard and life doesn't make sense.

- Devote ourselves in **prayer**, remain **watchful,** and give **thanks.**

- Learn to trust like a **child** with no hands on the handlebars.

What are you thankful for today?

_____
_____
_____
_____
_____
_____
_____

*Dear Lord, thank You for a wonderful week learning that when I am A-ligned to Your will I will have the power to accomplish amazing things for Your glory! Lead me and guide me as I humble myself and surrender my plans to You. I pray I take the time to sit and study Your Word so I might have the vision, conviction, and strength to ride into my days. Reveal to me Your Spirit—**personally**. Reveal to me your plan—**purposefully**. Reveal to me Your power—**passionately**. Today is a beautiful day for a bike ride. Amen.*

ESTHER's JOURNAL

• What decision do you need to make in this situation?	• If you were in control, what actions would you take?	• Because God is in control, how are you going to obey His leading?	• Write down God's faithfulness in this situation

A-lignment is essential for Riding Tandem. God has durable qualities to help us stay in A-lignment and not tandem topple.

We will learn THREE things about our A-lignment.

1. Are we _____ of A-lignment?
2. How do we get _____ into A-lignment?
3. How do we _____ in A-lignment?

1. Are we out of A-lignment?

• To search means: examined thoroughly, to be _____ out.

"Investigate my life, O God, find out everything about me; Cross-examine and test me, get a clear picture of what I'm about; See for yourself whether I've done anything wrong— then guide me on the road to eternal life."

Psalm 139:23-24

(MSG)

2. How do we get back into A-lignment?

• To get back into A-lignment, we have to identify what takes us _____ of A-lignment.
• Paul tells us that in order to stay A-ligned, we need to forget what is _____ and press on toward the goal to win the prize (Philippians 4:13-14).

3. How do we stay in A-lignment?

• While our destination is heaven, our goal is to _____ Jesus personally everyday.

Answers: out, back, stay, found, out, behind, know

A-lignment is about knowing God so He can:
Reveal His Spirit personally. Reveal His plan purposefully. Reveal His power passionately.

Week three is about N-ecessary Stops. While A-lignment is essential to balance us on our ride with Jesus, taking N-ecessary Stops gives us time to regroup, slow down, and reassess the direction we are headed.

However, some of us don't like to stop (ahem, me). Others don't feel they have time to stop because their lives are so hurry-hurry. The only problem with this riding strategy is that we will miss Jesus' work in our lives. We will become exhausted, over-stressed, and burned out. Remember, our Captain knows more about us than we do, and He knows when enough is enough. Here's my advice. When the Captain stops the bike, you better stop, too. Otherwise you are going to fly over the handlebars or find yourself pedaling ninety to nothin'—for nothin'. To have complete trust in our Captain, we have to have **complete trust** in His N-ecessary Stops.

Today, we are going to study Luke 24:13-35. To set the stage, Jesus has been arrested, crucified, and resurrected. Word is leaking out that some women, who were going to prepare the body with spices, found the tomb empty. We pick up the story and find two men walking to a village called Emmaus. While talking about everything that had just happened, Jesus comes up and walks **with them**, and yet they do not recognize Him.

Read Luke 24:13-35.

What do you think the men were discussing when Jesus walked beside them?

_____

_____

What was the overall demeanor of the men? (Luke 24:17)

_____

_____

Why do you think Jesus wanted a re-cap of all that was happening?

_____

_____

What was the hope of these two men? (Luke 24:21)

_____

_____

What was the final response of Jesus? (Luke 24:25-26)

_____

_____

What was the clue that opened their eyes to reveal it was actually Jesus who was with them all the time? (Luke 24:30-32)

_____

_____

N-ecessary Stops give us eyes to see with a **new perspective**. When we are walking too fast or preoccupied with our own agendas, we can't see our Captain right in front of us! Just ask these two men walking to Emmaus. I love what Jesus says to them in verse 25. The word for foolish comes from the Greek word "morosh," and it's where we get the word moron. Not what you expect your Captain to lean back and call you, right? But I bet it would get your attention! It got mine.

Here's what struck me. These men **knew** the words of the prophets. Good grief! They probably memorized the words of the Torah as boys. But because they were walking in their own opinions of what happened, they were distracted from the truth. These men thought Jesus was going to save them from the oppression of Rome and come forth as a King to rescue them. They had it all wrong. Jesus did come to save and He was a King, but He did not come to rescue Israel from political tyranny. He came to save us from the destitution of our sins. The freedom Jesus was offering was more than a freedom from Rome. It was a freedom from the chains of sin and separation from God. His death on the cross paid the penalty of our brokenness that began ALL the way back with the disobedience of Adam and Eve.

Here's what else struck me in the story. TIME. Can you imagine the time it took for Jesus to start at the beginning and tell the **whole** story from Moses and all the Prophets concerning Himself? I would guess about seven miles. What a great question to ponder while considering the **N-ecessary Stops** in Riding Tandem. We need to **stop** and **walk** with Jesus. He's got all the time in the world! Here's the best part. Jesus cares enough to stop us not only when our faith gets "cattywhompus," but also to teach us, counsel us, and steer us in the right direction.

Why do you think Jesus appeared to these two men to walk alongside and spend the next seven miles explaining His story?

_____

_____

_____

_____

Read Luke 18:31-33.

What was prophesied that Jesus had to endure?

_____

_____

What does Scripture say in Luke 18:34?

_____

_____

How does this parallel with Luke 24:16?

_____

_____

What significant event happened in Luke 24:30-32?

_____

_____

> "When he was at the table with them, he took bread, gave thanks, broke it and began to give it to them. Then their eyes were opened and they recognized him, ...They asked each other, "Were not our hearts burning within us while he talked with us on the road and opened the Scriptures to us?"
> Luke 24:30-32

Jesus told His disciples **all** that He must endure to fulfill the writings of the prophets, yet they did not understand and the meaning was held from them. Many commentators believe the disciples were too focused on Jesus' glory and the temporary Kingdom on earth to digest the reality of what He had to suffer. Others believe they were just plain ignorant. After all, He did call them foolish. Some believe they just could not understand. Here's what I took away from these Scriptures as a mom of four, a wife, a friend, and a keeper of laundry and ordinary household chores: Sometimes I don't always understand God's Word either. Let's give the disciples some grace. Sometimes I might hear something that makes no sense at the time, but later it makes **perfect sense**. Maybe we don't always have to understand. Maybe it might be too much for us to comprehend.

Daley was just 18-months old when she tripped on her blanket and busted her forehead wide open. She was in the nursery at BSF (Bible Study Fellowship) while I was listening to the lecture. I saw an assistant approach the podium, but I never imagined my named to be called. "Annie, you are immediately needed in the back of the sanctuary." My heart started racing. When I saw her poor little head, I immediately wrapped her in my arms and rushed to the pediatrician. They suggested I call a plastic surgeon because she **was** a girl and the slash **was** front and center. Dear me. Because the surgery was set for 4:00 that afternoon, we went home and Daley took a nap. As she slept peacefully, she did not need to know that in three hours she was going to be held down while they stitched her up. I call this God's mercy and grace. She did **not need to know** the future fear that would strike her as they took her from my arms. **She did not need to know**. She would not have understood and the meaning was held from her.

On the other hand, I DID know, and I was a nervous wreck! God showed me that day that I don't need to know or understand everything, especially the future. Honestly, I don't think any of us could personally handle the knowledge of knowing what is about to happen. Jesus knew this of the disciples, too. He knew there would be a time when they would get it. He knew the perfect timing would be at dinner when He broke the bread and gave thanks. Then their eyes would be opened to see Jesus and understand who He was and why He had to come. It would all make sense.

This is why I believe N-ecessary Stops are so important. They **open our eyes** to see Jesus. When we don't understand why things are happening, I think we like to put our own spin to it. When we are disappointed in the way life is turning out, we like to try to take control or believe in the opinions of others. And, as politically correct or socially acceptable as it may seem, it might not be the truth. This is dangerous territory. Be careful. To understand the truth of Scripture, we need to stop and take lots of walks with Jesus. When we speed through life, four things can happen:

- We miss seeing Jesus right in front of us.
- We forget God's promises.
- The truth is distorted.
- We believe what we want to believe (even if it opposes Scripture)
- This is a bonus: We will be called morons.

Seriously? I do not want to be a moron. This means I need to take N-ecessary Stops and spend time with Jesus. While we can't walk with Jesus physically anymore, we can read His Word and be inspired by the Holy Spirit. The same Jesus that showed up at dinner is living inside of us (Romans 8:10-11). We, too, can sense the same overwhelming power. "Were not our hearts burning within us while he talked with us on the road and opened the Scriptures to us?"

Jesus is so cool. I want to go on a seven mile walk with Him. I love that He has the time for me to do this. The question is, do I?

Today, He is waiting for you. He longs to teach you and explain His story. He wants to show you all His promises so when you SEE them, your heart will burn within you. Don't be distracted by the world's opinions. Seek His wisdom and it will be graciously given to you (James 1:3). Take the clues of N-ecessary Stops and stop pedaling. He has so much to teach us, but first we need to slow down, get off the bike, and listen. He's right beside you.

Dear Lord, thank You for teaching me about N-ecessary Stops this week. Why is it so hard to stop, Lord? I think it's because deep down I like the activity and often feel more worthy when I am busy. Thank You for opening my eyes to see that I need stops to walk with You. I need stops to talk with You. I need stops to change my perspective. I need stops to distinguish between public opinion and truth. Allow me to recognize YOU this week and to remember Your promises. Thank You for the freedom to not always understand, but to know that You are always walking beside me. Open my heart and my eyes to recognize You, today. Amen.

Last February, our family went to Disney World. As I approached the front of a very long line, a Disney employee took me aside and said, "Are you a Florida resident? Wait here."

As I was waiting, six other people went ahead of me! I was just about to express my opinion about being hoodwinked when the nice Disney man took me to a back window and said with a smile, **"It's quicker to wait."**

What on earth? As I left the line with my Animal Kingdom pass, I couldn't get his comment out of my head. It's quicker to wait? I don't think so Mr. Disney worker. But as I chewed on his comment for a while, I began to think that Smiley had a good point.

I love the **Streams in the Desert** devotion for May 17th:

> "The hours spent waiting are not lost time. Quite often God will ask us to wait before we go, so we may fully recover from our last mission before entering the next stage of our journey and work."[1]

I call this a N-ecessary Stop. Far too often we want to jump into the next activity, the next volunteer job, or the next obligation. But sometimes, God wants us to pause and take a break. Maybe He wants us to stop and wait. Because if it's not God's timing, you will waste your time. **It's quicker to wait.**

Ask Abraham.

Abram left his country and his people to go to the land the Lord would show him (Genesis 12:1-8). His Captain had set the direction and Abram was pedaling along for the ride not knowing what was ahead. I call this "Going and Not Knowing" (but that's another lesson!). God made many promises to Abram, including making him into a great nation and passing on the land to Abram's offspring. The only problem was that Abram and Sarai (later to be renamed Abraham and Sarah) did not have any children and the clock was ticking. They were both getting old, too old to bear children. So, instead of being quick to wait, Abram and Sarai decided to take matters in their own hands and ride right past the will of God.

Let's read Genesis 16:1-6.

What did Sarai suggest Abram do since she could not conceive?

_____

_____

What was Abram's decision?

_____

_____

What was the result? Do you think Sarai regretted her decision? How do we know this?

_____

_____

This is crazy, right? Through the story of Abram and Sarai, we get to see firsthand what happens when we decide that the promises made to us aren't meeting our deadlines or our expectations. We step out and make things happen. In our own way. In our own timing. In our complete control. But the result is a complete **bike wreck**.

Sarai ends up despising her maidservant to the point of abuse. Abram ends up with the famous line, "You told me to do it." The chains are off the bike. The brakes are not stopping the fast forward motion toward disaster and reality T.V. is filming the first episode.

I remember the day in kindergarten when Gareth Bond dared me to bite him. "What?" I said. "You're kidding, right?" "Nope," Gareth teased. **"I don't think you will do it."** SO—with a super strong will and a harder bite, I took a chunk out of his arm. He screamed to high heaven, told the teacher, and I was sent to the Principal's office for the first time in my life. My reason? He told me to do it! It wasn't a solid excuse for me, and it wasn't a solid excuse for Abraham. Taking matters into your own hands without consulting God is never a good idea.

Read the following verses. What does God teach us about the days of our lives? (I promise I didn't mean to type that. How funny! Maybe that's where they got the first soap opera title!)

- **Proverbs 16:9**

"In his heart a man plans his course, but the Lord determines his steps."

_____
_____
_____

- **Psalm 90:12**

_____
_____
_____

- **Psalm 39:4**

_____
_____
_____

- **Psalm 139:15-16**

_____
_____
_____

We can plan, plan, plan, or bite, bite, bite all we want, but it is the Lord who determines our steps and STOPS.

N-ecessary Stops **to believe** in the promises of God
N-ecessary Stops **to know** that God has ordained each day for us.
N-ecessary Stops **to ask** for wisdom because life is short.

We have one opportunity to ride this tandem through life. We can either ride alone or ask the Captain to be our leader and direct us each day. Yesterday, we looked at what happens when our own agendas and plans become our focus. We can't even see or recognize that Jesus is walking with us. Today we see from Scripture what happens when we try to grip the handlebars and steer our own direction. We miss out on God's promises and mess up the plan. But the BEST part of this learning process is that we also find that our Captain **loves to rescue.** It's what He was sent to do! The most exciting part in this story (and our stories) is that God, our Captain, never gives up on us—even after a bike wreck leaves us broken, banged up, and bleeding.

Let's continue reading Genesis 17:1-8, 15-22.

What does God tell Abram again? (Genesis 17:1-8) *note: God changes Abram's name to Abraham in verse 5.*

_____

_____

What was the promise? (Genesis 12:1-3, Genesis 13:14-16)

_____

_____

How old were Abraham and Sarah? (Genesis 17:17) *note: God changes Sarai's name to Sarah in verse 15.*

_____

_____

What does God tell Abraham about Sarah? (Genesis 17:19)

_____

_____

How did God bless Ishmael?

_____

_____

I love the King James Version translation for Genesis 17:2 written in the side bar. It rhymes! The NIV uses the word **confirm** for the word **make**. It tells us that God confirmed the covenant. The word for make/confirm is **nathan**. It means: to give, bestow, grant, permit, devote, dedicate, lend, commit, entrust, give over, assign.[2] This is important because we see God giving, entrusting, and confirming His covenant (God's promise) to Abraham.

From Genesis 16:16, we read that Abram was 86 when Ishmael was born. Genesis 17:1 tells us Abram was 100 when Isaac was born. That's 14 years in the small space between these two verses and a 14 year **N-ecessary Stop** to get Abraham's alignment back in balance. I see many lessons in the spaces of these two verses. Here are two.

> • God allows time to heal our past mistakes.
> • God never turns His back on His promises.

> "And I will make my covenant between me and thee, and will multiply thee exceedingly."
> Genesis 17:2 (KJV)

It's the stops in life that allow us to review and receive God's grace. When we stop long enough, our eyes are opened to know that only by God's power can miracles happen. Goodness. Abraham and Sarah were old. Really old—too old to have children. Only God could have opened Sarah's womb and made her able to conceive. And only God can rescue us from our past mistakes and give us another chance. **Only God.** Why? Because when He makes a promise, He's committed. He's all in. And, when our N-ecessary Stop is over, He confirms His love for us and entrusts us with His plans, again and again. He holds the bike steady, forgives us, and invites us to Ride Tandem.

I don't know if Gareth ever forgave me for biting him. But God sure did.

I'm back on the bike and riding—again.

LEAD ME

Lesson Three/ UNTIL MOMENTS

N-ecessary Stops are essential to our ride on the tandem bike.
Here's another reason why.

When we slow down to stop, we can look into our past and **see** where God has been faithful. This is especially important when the road ahead seems dim. To press ahead, God wants us to remember His faithfulness. Necessary Stops help us to slow down to see that He was there all along. Unfortunately, our tendency can be to take quick glances into our rear view mirror when life is full steam ahead. The problem is this: Steam on the mirror makes it too foggy to see God's blessings in our lives.

About two years ago my husband, Curry, shared that He believed God wanted him to look at another job opportunity. That's when you hold your breath and say with kindness, "Great. Let's talk about this." Or with a smile, deliver this one liner, "It's quicker to wait!" Just kidding. The crazy part about this conversation was that the job position was not even open. Still, he felt led to pursue the path with gusto. About this time, I was reading *Circle Maker* by Mark Batterson. It's a book about circling your dreams. Never quitting. Praying through. Praying hard. It's about seeking out what God has placed in your heart. (This book is tremendous, and I highly recommend it!)

Knowing this journey might be tough for him, I made Curry a postcard and taped it to the mirror in our bathroom where he could see it everyday. From Deuteronomy 2:7 (HCSB), I wrote:

"For the LORD your God has blessed you, Curry, in all the work of your hands. He has watched over your journey through this immense wilderness. The LORD your God has been with you, Curry, this past 40 years, and you have lacked nothing.'"

While this verse speaks specifically to Moses, I wanted Curry to take a **N-ecessary Stop** and look into his rear view mirror often. My prayer for him was to **remember** that God had blessed the work of his hands, had always been with him, and had never let him lack anything. That's an important reminder when you are about to step into unknown territory. Stopping allows us to be intentional and **remember** God's goodness **before** we ride into uncharted waters. He didn't leave us then, and He won't leave us now.

How has God blessed you, watched over your journey, and saw that you lacked for nothing?

_____
_____
_____
_____
_____
_____

God is with us in this tandem ride through life. Remember, this bicycle is built for two. Moses' journey shows us that as he traveled 40 years in the wilderness with a crazy crew of emotional Israelites, God's hand of provision and protection never left them—EVEN in their disobedience (not willing to go into the promised land) and EVEN through their grumbling and complaining. God's hand never left the handlebars. I love God's patience and overwhelming love for His people. I need it all the time!

Open your Bibles. Read Exodus 15:11-13 and Exodus 16:1-16.

How do the Israelite's extol the Lord in Exodus 15:11?

_____

_____

_____

How does the Israelite's attitude change in Exodus 16:3? What do they think of God in this verse? Why?

_____

_____

_____

How did God continue to provide for them after some serious hissy fits?

_____

_____

_____

Whining. Grumbling. Complaining. As if it were yesterday, I remember my dad pulling the car over because of four girls complaining in the back seat. And, if you happen to be counting seat belts (which we did not have or use), I was in the trunk space of our station wagon—and thankful for it. I was not as easy to reach. Ah, the benefit of being the baby.

The Israelites were experts at complaining. Just one chapter before the grumbling, they were pontificating about the majesty and wonder of the Lord **until** their comforts were challenged. The word **until** spoke loud and clear to me.

They were delighting in the Lord . . . **until** their stomachs gurgled.
They were praising God for all His glory . . . **until** they were uncomfortable.

Do you honestly think the Israelites wanted to go back into slavery and suppression under Pharaoh? No way. These until moments are good N-ecessary Stops for all of us to consider. Why? They test the foundation of our faith.

Have you had an UNTIL moment in your life? One minute you are praising the Lord for all of His glory. Life is great. God is great. And, the next minute you are not so sure He even cares.

_____

_____

_____

_____

_____

God was my rock and foundation, UNTIL my husband told me I didn't matter anymore.

God was always there for me, UNTIL I was diagnosed.

God was my song, UNTIL I lost my job.

Whatever your UNTIL moment, today is a good reason to stop. **God is with you.** N-ecessary Stops help us evaluate and remember that God is indeed good. As Deuteronomy suggests, He has blessed us. He is with us. He is providing all that we need, and He is **forever faithful.**

Hebrews 11:1 defines **faith.**

When we cannot SEE God at work, faith sees for us. We have hope and conviction that our Captain is taking us to the place He desires us to be. It's not always the destination God is concerned about, but rather the **journey to get us there.** This is where real life lessons are learned.

"Now faith is the assurance
of things hoped for,
the conviction
of things not seen."
Hebrews 11:1

How can the following verses remind us that God is faithful in the UNTIL moments?

- **Psalm 86:15**

"But you, O Lord, are a God merciful and gracious, slow to anger and abounding in steadfast love and faithfulness." Psalm 86:15

_____
_____

- **Deuteronomy 7:9**

_____
_____

- **1 Corinthians 1:9**

"God is faithful, by whom you were called into the fellowship of his Son, Jesus Christ our Lord." 1 Corinthians 1:9

_____
_____

- **1 Corinthians 10:13**

_____
_____

As we close for today, print out this card (go to www.thouartexalted.com/riding-tandem) and remember that God is your Captain in your **UNTIL moments.** Treasure this time of stillness to fill up and remember His promises.

Dear Lord, thank You that You are indeed faithful. Even when I cannot see the road clearly, I know You are my Captain and are steering my tandem bike. You are steadfast when I am shaky. You are full of mercy when I am meandering. You are leading when I am lopsided. Give me the desire to slow down and take a good look into my past where I can see Your unswerving guidance. Remind me each morning, that You are leading me into Your ways. And, Lord, when I have those UNTIL moments, please steady the bike for me. Help me to remember Deuteronomy 2:7. You have blessed me. You are with me. You have given me work to do with my hands. You have never left my side, and I have never lacked anything. You are my Captain. Let's enjoy this stop together. Amen.

When we cannot see God at work, faith sees for us.

Today, we are going to back pedal a little. There are just too many lessons the Israelites experienced in their UNTIL moments not to go back and learn from them.

There are three things we will learn today from the N-ecessary Stop God made the Israelites take. I think we will all be able to identify.

1. Hunger exaggerates complaining.

Open your Bible and read Exodus 16:3 again. In your opinion, why would this statement be a bit exaggerated?

_____

_____

_____

_____

_____

Empty stomachs magnify our emotions—at least they do in our family! Empty stomachs make us "hangry"(a combination of hungry and angry). On a side note, I am convinced that all children (including the Israelites) have the universal middle name "starving." Mine do!

"Hi John John. How was your day?" **I'm starving.**
"Great to see you Curry, Jr.! How was football?" **I'm starving.**
"Winnie, how was ballet?" **I'm starving.**
"Daley! How was the Bible Study with the girls?" **I'm starving.**

And, of course, if your house is like ours, there is never ANYTHING to eat. Don't get me wrong. I am not trying to be hard on my kids. When I am hungry, my emotions tend to reach a high level, too. How about you?

2. God continues to provide for us even when we complain.

Reread Exodus 16:4 and visualize the overwhelming compassion of the Lord.

Amazing! God hears our complaining and STILL provides all that we need. The NIV translation says, "they will gather enough for that day." Notice this verse does not say everything they **wanted**. Big difference. Goodness. If God gave the Israelites what they wanted, they would be back eating all they desired in Egypt (vs. 3). Maybe hunger makes us hallucinate, too—making our past look dreamy and magical. Warning: This is a ploy of the enemy. His purpose from the beginning of time has been to get us to believe that God is not good enough. Don't be lured into his web of lies. **God is enough. He will ALWAYS be enough.** He will continue to rain down His compassion on us. Every day. All day.

Take that Satan!

> "Then the Lord said to Moses, 'I will rain down bread from heaven for you. Everyday the people must go out and gather what they NEED for the day." Exodus 16:4 (NLT)

N-ecessary Stops help us to identify the lies.

Read the following verses. What is the TRUTH about God providing what we need and not necessarily what we want?

• Psalm 23:1-3

_____
_____
_____

• Philippians 4:19

_____
_____
_____

• 2 Corinthians 9:8

_____
_____
_____

"And God will generously provide all you need. Then you will always have everything you need and plenty left over to share with others."
2 Corinthians 9:8 (NLT)

The Lord is our Shepherd and our Captain. He knows what we need and will not leave us on the side of the road. He protects us and will generously provide **enough** for us. In fact, He will supply so much that we will have leftovers! I needed to hear this today. I also needed to hear that God's love is not conditional. My behavior never tips the scale of His unconditional love for me. He never thinks, "Well, it looks like Annie is trying to steer her circumstances again, I think I'll just opt-out for sending her compassion today." No way. This is not God's nature. God's love never changes. It is unconditional. Read Psalm 145:9.

"The LORD is good to everyone. He showers compassion on all his creation." Psalm 145:9 (NLT)

YES. Even in our sinful, complaining, over-exaggerating, selfish-selves, **GOD is still good**. He is still showering His compassion on ALL His creation. One of my favorite art projects I have created comes from one of my tween Bible studies called The Perfect Present. In the first lesson, we study God's character with the acronym of G.I.F.T.— God is **G**-reat. God is **I**-nfinite. God is our **F**-ather. And God is **T**-ruth. The art project for the day? Umbrellas! Why? Because God showers His compassion on all His creation!

3. Knowing and Seeing.

This third point might seem a bit obscure to learn from Israel's N-ecessary Stop, but when we reread Exodus 16:6-7, you will see the direction we are headed.

"So Moses and Aaron said to all the men, 'This evening you will KNOW that the Lord is the one who brought you out of Egypt. Tomorrow morning you will SEE the greatness of the Lord."

Even in the wilderness of the Israelite's complaining and over-exaggeration, the Lord rained down compassion by giving them manna in the morning and quail in the evening. Can you imagine the miracle? In this stop, they experienced the greatness of the Lord. They **knew** the greatness. They **saw** the greatness. **Knowing and seeing—** exactly in that order. This is imperative to our lesson—and our **N-ecessary Stop.**

My question for us is this: What will it take for us to KNOW God? I am not talking about knowing about Him, but rather knowing Him personally and experientially, like my sister (week two, A-lignment). We need to know that God is enough, and that He abundantly provides for our every need. We need to know Him enough . . .

- **To stop** our complaining.
- **To trust** Him in the "I'm hungry" times.
- **To believe** in His goodness in the "I don't understand" times.
- **To have the faith** to know that God is steering our tandem bike when we hit those "UNTIL" moments.
- **To identify** the truth from the lies.

What will it take for us to KNOW God? Will it take a miracle? Walking on water? Watching an ocean part so we can cross on dry land? Will it take watching food appear in the morning and evening to satisfy our hunger? Even in these amazing mountaintop moments when God displayed His power, the Israelites lost faith. We will, too. All they wanted in their UNTIL moment was to return to the valley of exaggerated complaining, believing they were better off not having been rescued at all. Do we lose faith this quickly? How do we react when God allows a difficult season in our lives?

I am always moved when I hear Lauren Daigles's song, *Trust in You*.[3] Take a N-ecessary Stop and download this song onto your playlist. For now, enjoy these few lines:

> Truth is you know what tomorrow brings
> There's not a day ahead you have not seen
> So let all things be my life and breath
> I want what you want Lord and nothing less
>
> When you don't move the mountains
> I'm needing you to move
> When you don't part the waters
> I wish I could walk through
> When you don't give the answers
> As I cry out to you
> I will trust, I will trust, I will trust in you
> I will trust in you

Until we **KNOW** our Captain and believe in His strength, power, love, compassion, and desire for us to get us where He wants us to go, we will not **SEE** nor understand why or where He is leading us. Jesus said, "I am the bread of life. Whoever comes to me will never go hungry, and whoever believes in me will never be thirsty" (John 6:35). We might not have manna in the morning and quail in the evening, but we do have the Word of God to sustain us. We never have to be hangry again. God commands us not to complain or argue (Philippians 2:14). This is why we need N-ecessary Stops. We have to FILL up with God's promises so that when we hit those hangry, complaining, until, "mountains-don't-move" moments, we have God's Word to speak into those empty places.

> "Then Jesus declared, 'I am the bread of life. Whoever comes to me will never go hungry, and whoever believes in me will never be thirsty.'"
> John 6:35

51

As we close, consider this. Are you hungry for something the Lord has not given to you? Has a mountain not moved in your life? Is your appetite for more consuming your thoughts? Or, are you satisfied with the provision He has given you?

_____

_____

_____

_____

_____

_____

_____

_____

_____

_____

_____

Dear Lord, thank You for Your overflowing compassion for Your children. Even in my rotten attitude, You continue to love me. I pray that today's N-ecessary Stop will open my eyes to the truth of Your Word and will destroy the lies that invade my mind. The truth of Your Word is the best weapon I have to fight my "hangry" dispositions, bitter heart, and complaining attitudes. My desire is to KNOW You and to SEE the evidence of Your hand in my life. I, like sheep, have gone astray, and I know I'm not the smartest of creatures. Help me to understand that You are enough. Show me Your provision in my life, today. Open my eyes to see the wonderful! Amen.

Lesson Five/ UNCOMMON WEAPONS

N-ecessary Stops are never intended so that we can have an excuse to quit or give up. No. N-ecessary Stops are meant to refresh our spirit and reflect on God's faithfulness.

Stops are to open our eyes, slow us down, correct our A-lignment, and **refocus.** Sometimes we can be headed in the wrong direction when Jesus comes up, walks beside us, and turns us around. Sometimes we can say the wrong thing or make a serious mistake. We **need** N-ecessary Stops to examine and evaluate our hiccups. They may take 14 years (like Abram) or 4 days. The purpose behind a stop is to listen, be still, and ask for God's wisdom and grace for a new start. When we do, we begin to **SEE** differently.

- **We will see God's plan** and purpose for our lives.
- **We will see God's hope** in a hopeless situation.
- **We will see God's compassion** in our complaining.
- **We will see God's TRUTH**.
- **We will receive God's grace** and renewed gumption to get back on the bike and ride again.

N-ecessary Stops give us new eyes to see God at work. But how can we see with God's perspective? He gives us **uncommon weapons** to fight common battles. It may not be easy. It may take discipline and hard work. But it's worth it. Remember, riding tandem is about the journey.

Winnie was stuck, and it was clearly her fault. She was curious to see if she could wedge her arm in between the rod iron bars on the elementary school playground. **Wedge she did. Stuck she was.** Panic hit and her friends started laughing at her. To cover up her embarrassment, she laughed with them while at the same time wondering how in the world she was going to get her arm out. When the bell rang, she knew she needed help. Ron, the head security guard, just smiled at my daughter and said, "Winnie, Oh Winnie. Hang tight. I've got an idea!" When he came out with a slab of butter, Winnie's eyes got really big! "Butter? Mr. Ron, do you really think this will work?" she questioned. Mr. Ron greased a slab of butter on Winnie's arm and with ease, her arm slid right out. Uncommon solutions in sticky situations work every time.

I've been waiting three weeks to share this with you. This is so exciting! Let's turn to the good ole' story of David and Goliath. We are going to learn how to fight sticky situations with **uncommon solutions** and battles with **uncommon weapons.** Get ready. These are not the conventional weapons of this world. They are God's weapons.

Read 1 Samuel 17:17-58.

What did David's brothers say to him? What names did they call him? (1 Samuel 17:28)

_____

_____

What was King Saul's response to David? (1 Samuel 17:33)

_____

_____

How did Goliath try to humiliate David? (1 Samuel 17:41-44)

_____

_____

What did David say in response to ALL these discouraging remarks? (1 Samuel 17:26, 34-37, 45-47)

_____

_____

_____

One brother, one king, and one giant tried to discourage David from fighting Goliath.

Before we learn the uncommon weaponry, what would you have used to fight back in this situation? Anger? Foul language? Irritability? Attitude?

_____

_____

_____

_____

I think I would have been furious. If my big sisters picked on me like that, especially when I was trying to do something good, you better bet I would have fought back with harsh words and an attitude. Not David. Conventional weaponry was not in his arsenal. He had a mission. God's mission. One might think that his smooth stones and a simple sling shot won the battle. But they would be wrong. David had the most powerful weapon in the Book. **God's Word.** With every discouraging comment, David fought back with the power of God's promises. David spoke God's Word to his brothers, King Saul, and Goliath. He proclaimed that God has an army (vs. 26,45), God is a LIVING God (vs. 26), and that God will deliver the faithful (vs. 37,46). **God's promises are the uncommon weapons.**

Jesus used the same weaponry when He was tempted by the devil in Matthew 4.

Read Matthew 4:1-11. I love how the New Living Translation translates Jesus' responses.

Matthew 4:4

"But Jesus told him, "No! **The Scriptures say**, 'People do not live by bread alone, but by every word that comes from the mouth of God.'"

Matthew 4:7

Jesus responded, "**The Scriptures also say**, 'You must not test the Lord your God.'"

Matthew 4:10

"Get out of here, Satan," Jesus told him. "**For the Scriptures say**, 'You must worship the Lord your God and serve only him.'"

What is the repeating phrase? Yes. "For the Scriptures say . . ." Did you also notice that Satan knew the Scriptures, too?

Read the following by John Eldridge from his daily devotional *Ransomed Heart*:

"In order to recognize a lie, we need to know the truth. Experts in counterfeit money don't spend their time studying counterfeits. They study the real currency. In the same way, to engage in the spiritual battle raging around us, we don't shift our focus to lies or to the Devil. We focus on Jesus. We marinate in the truth of who God is and who he says we are. Then and only then will we be able to quickly recognize a lie."[4]

If we don't take N-ecessary Stops to study the truth, we will never be able to identify the counterfeit and fight back with God's true promises. Satan knows Scripture well enough to tweak it just enough to make it false and deceive us to believe it's real. If we don't know the **truth**, we can be dissuaded by **counterfeit truth.**

Have you ever bought a fake brand-name purse? Fess up. At least I will (to make you feel better!). I bought a fake purse in the early 90's. It looked so real. It felt 100% genuine. People also thought I had forked out a lot of money to buy this purse. **UNTIL** . . . the sticker started coming off. Oh, the embarrassment. Here's my take away. Satan's lies may appear as real as the truth, but his sticker will eventually fall off, too. **He's not the truth.** He's the big fat ugly giant trying to tell you that you can't win the battle and life is hopeless. Remember, Satan will always try to convince you that God is not enough. When we know the truth of Scripture, we can fight back with God's Promises.

What giants are you facing today? Anger? A broken marriage? Past mistakes? Pride? Future decisions? Job related issues?

_____
_____
_____
_____
_____
_____

What are you afraid of? Sickness? Loneliness? Embarrassment? Has God given you a N-ecessary Stop to stock up on some Scripture? Take a minute to identify the giants in your life.

_____

_____

_____

_____

_____

_____

Let's look up some uncommon weaponry that we can use in our battles against giants. What are the uncommon weapons used to fight our battles?

• **Colossians 3:13-14**

_____

_____

• **Psalm 103:10**

"He does not treat us as our sins deserve or repay us according to our iniquities." Psalm 103:10

_____

_____

• **Joshua 1:9**

_____

_____

• **Psalm 13:5**

_____

_____

These promises are just a fragment of God's arsenal. Don't use the weapons of anger, force, or manipulation to fight your battles. Instead, search the Word of God and ask the Holy Spirit to guide you in choosing the right one.

• When someone hurts you, fight back with **forgiveness.**

"Make allowance for each other's faults, and forgive anyone who offends you. Remember, the Lord forgave you, so you must forgive others." Colossians 3:13 (NLT)

• When someone mistreats you, fight back with **God's mercy.**

"He does not treat us as our sins deserve or repay us according to our iniquities." Psalm 103:10

• When you are facing a giant, fight back with **courage.**

"Have I not commanded you? Be strong and courageous. Do not be terrified; do not be discouraged, for the LORD your God will be with you wherever you go." Joshua 1:9

- When a situation is not going the direction you intended, fight back with **love.**

  "But I trust in your unfailing love; my heart rejoices in your salvation. Psalm 13:5

- When your arm gets caught in the railing, fight back with **butter.** (I couldn't find a verse for that one!)

The good news is this: Jesus has already won the battle. We need to lean into His leading and trust in His protection and direction for our lives. Every. Single. Day. Take N-ecessary Stops to know the TRUTH of Scripture. Don't allow the sticker to fall off your bike. You have the **real** promise. The **real** hope. The **real** Jesus. When someone says something hurtful, fight back with the uncommon weapons of God's promises.

I love the song, *The Voice Of Truth*, from Casting Crowns about fighting our fears. Read these lyrics.[5]

> But the voice of truth tells me a different story
> And the voice of truth says, "Do not be afraid!"
> And the voice of truth says, "This is for My glory"
> Out of all the voices calling out to me
>
> I will choose to listen and believe
> I will choose to listen and believe the voice of truth

N-ecessary Stops are necessary. They stop us to reassess, reevaluate, and remember that God is good. They slow us down to see Jesus walking beside us. They quiet our hearts to wait for God's perfect timing. They remind us that God is always there for us in those until moments. They expose our hangry, complaining, unthankful souls to change our perspective. They allow us to fill up on the power of God's Word so we can distinguish the truth from the lies. **They give us uncommon weaponry.**

My prayer is that we will take regular N-ecessary Stops. Be on the alert when Jesus is slowing down the bike so you can get off and take a breather. It is worth it. He can make up the time. When we are rested, we can hop on the back and ride with the confidence that Jesus, our Captain, has already won the battle.

Great job this week! **In closing, write a prayer** and tell God what you have learned about N-ecessary Stops. Write the promises you will use as You trust Him to fight your battles for you. I'll start with a favorite.

"The LORD will fight for you; you need only to be still **(and take N-ecessary Stops!)**." Exodus 14:14

_____

_____

_____

_____

_____

_____

_____

_____

_____

_____

_____

_____

We will learn THREE things about N-ecessary Stops.

1. _____ do we stop?
2. _____ do we do when we stop?
3. _____ do we stop and what are the benefits when we stop?

1. When do we take a N-ecessary Stop?

• When life gets too busy, we can't see what's _____ _____ right in front of us.
• We stop when we realize that we have left _____ behind.

"After three days they found him in the temple courts, sitting among the teachers, listening to them and asking them questions."

Luke 2:46

2. What do we do in a N-ecessary Stop?

• Jesus was sitting among the teachers, _____ to them, and _____ questions.
• When we are in a crisis situation, the flurry of family, friends, opinions, and media can get us in a tight mess. We need to go back to the source. We need to go back to _____.

3. When do we stop? What are the benefits when we stop?

• Because the Lord is our Shepherd, we have everything we _____.

When we stop, God _____.
When we sit, God _____.
When we listen, God speaks _____ into our lives.
When we ask questions, God reaffirms His love for us and fills us with the desire to walk in _____.

Answers: When, What, Why, most important, Jesus, listening, asking, Jerusalem, need, intercedes, teaches, truth, obedience.

We are over the hump and riding into week four. D-on't Stop Pedaling. In review, we have prepared for T-akeoff, A-ligned ourselves correctly, and realized the need for N-ecessary Stopping points.

I must interject that Riding Tandem was not the original name for this study. The first title was **LEAD.** Simple and to the point. I am not sure why I was drawn to this word, but it seemed that LEAD was in every verse I was studying. Has this ever happened to you? If so, take note. I believe God is trying to tell you something! Lead is used over and over again in the Old and New Testament. God will LEAD us. We will LEAD others. Others will LEAD us. We are called LEADers—both good and bad. It's a fascinating word search.

So what does LEAD have to do with our fourth chapter, D-on't Stop Pedaling?
Let's take a look at our first verse and ride on.

Habakkuk 3:19 reads, "The Sovereign Lord is my strength; he makes my feet like the feet of a deer, he enables me to tread on the heights . . ." (NIV)

"The Lord God gives me my strength. He makes me like a deer, which does not stumble. He leads me safely on the steep mountains. For the director of music. On my stringed instruments."

Habakkuk 3:19 (ICB)

The Holman Christian Standard Bible says, "He **enables** me to walk on mountain heights!" but the International Children's Bible reads, "He **leads** me safely on the steep mountains . . . ." The word for enable is *darak* meaning to cause to or to LEAD.[1]

When you read the ICB translation of Habakkuk 3:19 in the margin, what two words pop out to you?

_____

_____

The two words that struck a cord for me were: STEEP and SAFELY. Makes you think, right? I am so glad God is leading!

Curry, Jr. was 7-years-old when he decided that his dad's directions down the mountain in Wyoming were not going to work for him. Why go up and away from the ranch when the direct path was down and to the right? Without asking permission, Curry, Jr. took off and blazed his own trail. By himself. My husband didn't budge, kept on walking, and let him go. I was not so calm. OK. I was freaking out. (In our family this is called a F.O. — a freak out!)

"Curry! You can't let a child go down a mountain by himself hoping he will make it back safely. It's steep, and who knows what is behind or in that sage bush," I argued. So, we split up. Not by choice. Curry, Sr. took Winnie and John-John. I took Daley, and we started hiking down the mountain to find Curry. Needless to say, I was NOT a happy camper at this point. Not happy for my husband. Not happy for my son. What a joy I was to hike with!

We finally found little Curry. He was clearly frustrated that the path he had chosen was thorny and ankle deep in mud. More than that, admitting that his dad was right was really frustrating. We sure can get upset when we know someone else's choice was better all along! It's a pride thing, and it starts early.

Curry, Sr. knew the way. He was our leader. He also had hiked this mountain many times before. Yes, he knew the path looked steeper at first, but in the end, it was the safest way to the finish line. **Steep and safe.**

Winnie and John-John were skipping into the ranch singing "Mr. Bluebirds on my shoulder." When Daley, Curry, and I hit the finish line, I was singing, "You better get your rear end in the shower." It's not a good song. But, then again, I was not in a good mood either. Joy.

Here's my point. Instead of following Curry, Sr. who knew the way, Curry Jr. hiked the path that seemed the quickest, easiest, and more direct. He found out very quickly that his decision was the wrong one. He should have followed his father.

According to Habakkuk 3:19, what does God give us when we follow His lead?

_____

_____

_____

How are we described?

_____

_____

_____

How does He LEAD us?

_____

_____

_____

I consider steep mountains to be those difficult times in our lives when we are at a crossroads. We can choose to go our own way on a path that may seem more direct, easy, and quick. Or, we can choose to take a N-ecessary Stop and ask God for directions. The one credit I will give to little Curry was that he never gave up. He was pedaling for sure—but in his own power. That's never good. Pedaling on a tandem bike takes the work of both riders. Here is another amazing fact about the functionality of two people pedaling. There is more power! Have you ever tried to pedal alone on the back of a tandem while the front rider glides? It's near impossible, and not to mention **exhausting**.

God never intended for us to pedal alone. But, He did intend for us to pedal. We must press on and persevere through difficult times, not because we can pedal faster or harder, but because He is **helping** us pedal. Remember, He is our Duracell® power (chapter two, lesson one).

What do these verses say about allowing God to supply the power?

• **2 Chronicles 32:7**

"Be strong and courageous! Don't be afraid or discouraged because of the king of Assyria or his mighty army, for there is a power far greater on our side!" 2 Chronicles 32:7 (NLT)

_____

_____

_____

• **Psalm 118:8**

_____

_____

_____

• **Psalm 40:4**

_____

_____

_____

• **Matthew 19:26**

_____

_____

_____

• **Jeremiah 10:12**

_____

_____

_____

We will never make it through this life if we depend on our own abilities. We can muster up all the power and might we have to get through a difficult situation, but in the end, we will have muddy feet and frustrated hearts. When we trust in the Lord's power, He will make our feet like a deer who skips along the rocky edges of the mountains. We will have courage and strength when the path looks too steep to climb. We will be blessed with endurance to press on knowing we are safe in His arms. Although at first the path may seem higher and out of sight, TRUST in the Captain. He has hiked this mountain before. All things are possible with God.

As we close today, think about a time when you did it your own way and pedaled in your own strength. What happened? Think also about a time when you trusted in God. What was the difference?

_____

_____

_____

_____

_____

_____

Dear Lord, thank You that You are my Captain who gives me the strength to pedal through difficult situations. You are my power source and my refuge in times of trouble. Nothing is impossible for You. Give me the wisdom to trust in You for all areas of my life, especially those where I am trying to pedal all by myself. It's hard, exhausting, and, ultimately, a losing battle. Lead me today, O Lord, safely through the difficulty of steep mountainous situations. Whether at work, or at home, in relationships, in unfulfilled desires, or broken dreams—with You as my Leader, I am sure to find strength, safety, and protection. Lead me, Lord, and equip me with Your Spirit. Amen.

Lesson Two/ KEEP ON BELIEVING

Our elementary school has chapel every Thursday morning. This particular morning, Winnie was singing, so I was all eyes and ears.

But it was not Winnie that caught my attention (although I think she is pretty darn cute!). It was the song about **hope** written during the Nazi regime that resounded in my soul.

I still believe—in the darkness and in the loneliness. I still believe there is a God. I know this sounds super depressing, but it was beautiful. I wish there was a button on this page you could push and hear the sweet voices of these precious children. The tune of the song was just as gentle and convicting as the message. When I left chapel that morning, I was fully convinced that God's presence will always penetrate even the darkest of moments.

Let's examine the word LEAD again.

What do the following verses teach us about God's leading that guides us through the darkness of situations?

- **Isaiah 42:16**

_____

_____

- **Isaiah 49:10**

_____

_____

- **Isaiah 58:8,11**

_____

_____

- **Exodus 15:13**

"In your unfailing love you will lead the people you have redeemed. In your strength you will guide them to your holy dwelling." Exodus 15:13

_____

_____

- **Isaiah 58:10-11**

_____

_____

- **Proverbs 3:5-6**

"Trust in the LORD with all your heart; do not depend on your own understanding. Seek his will in all you do, and he will show you which path to take. Don't be impressed with your own wisdom. Instead, fear the LORD and turn away from evil." Proverbs 3:5-7 (NLT)

_____

_____

Which of these verses do you need to take to heart today? Could it be the promise that God will lead you on unfamiliar paths and make the rough places smooth? Do you need to be reminded again that God has compassion for you? Do you need His strength and guidance? Do you need to trust Him more and depend less on your own ideas and agendas? Do you need to believe that His light will break forth and dispel the darkness?

Use the space below to write a personal prayer telling God what you need today. Allow the power of these verses to lead you as you lean on Him.

_____
_____
_____
_____
_____
_____
_____

I rely on these verses quite often, both personally and professionally. ThouArtExalted Ministries didn't start overnight. It began with a simple idea to reach my daughter's struggles in 4th grade. The combination of using creativity to spread the Good News of the Gospel turned into a full blown non-profit ministry. I had no idea the road on which God was leading. Excited about the calling, I quickly found that ministry could be lonely and confusing at times. On numerous occasions, I felt too overwhelmed to keep going and wanted to quit and give up altogether. It was in these moments that I leaned on God's strength, compassion, guidance, and unfailing love. On a road I never thought I would be pedaling, He was and still is my Captain.

Looking more closely at Isaiah 58:8, we see that **God is before, behind, and with us.**

"Then your light will break forth like the dawn, and your healing will quickly appear; then your righteousness will go before you, and the glory of the LORD will be your rear guard. Then you will call, and the Lord will answer; You will call for help, and he will say: Here I am." Isaiah 58:8

This is wonderful news! God is with us, ahead of us, and behind us!

- God will break forth. He is in the **present** moment.
- God will go before you. He is going **ahead** of you.
- God will be your rear guard. He is **behind** you.

We all have blind spots in life. These are the moments you can't see that hit you out of nowhere. My encouragement to you is this: **D-on't Stop Pedaling.** Why? God will break forth, go before you, and come behind you. His vision trumps our blind spots every time.

In February, 2011, **I was done.** Why in the world was I trying to launch this ministry anyway? I was alone and under qualified. I was the "one-monkey-band" trying to fill all areas of ministry from writing to designing, editing to marketing, speaking to creating. I did not have a seminary degree, and I hadn't heard from the publishing house who was evaluating my study in months. I went to bed in tears believing the lies that Satan was enjoying planting in my feeble brain.

The next morning, I hesitantly opened my Bible to 2 Chronicles **29:11**. Pause: I had been writing a study for tween girls called Project **2911,** where verses from Scripture either had the address Chapter **29:11** or Chapter **2:9-11**. While 1 Chronicles **29:11** is the foundational verse for ThouArtExalted, I opened to 2 Chronicles **29:11** to see what promises it had to offer. Here is what I read. (I put my name in place of "my sons" to make it more personal.)

"My sons (Annie), do not be negligent now, for the Lord has chosen you to stand before him and to serve him, to minister before him, and to burn incense" (2 Chronicles 29:11).

My heart skipped a beat. Okay. It skipped several beats. Was this the light breaking through the darkness of my emotions? Was this the light showing me God did have a plan? Was this the light highlighting my path of uncertainty? **Yes.** This light was exposing my fears and filling it with compassion and unfailing love! God was answering my call for help. It was as if God whispered into my soul. *Here I am, Annie. Don't stop pedaling! I've got you. I want you to keep going. I will be your strength. Don't pedal in your own power or timing. Trust in Me. I want you to stand for ME. I want you to serve ME. I want you to minister and shine for ME.*

If that wasn't enough, that very afternoon God showed me another confirmation. I was picking up my daughter from school (the very daughter I started this ministry for in the first place), and the bridge that had been under construction was finally open. This is what the large blinking 10 x 5 foot sign read:

BRIDGE OPEN. 2-9-11.

HOLY COW! I stopped the car. What was the date? February 9th, 2011. **2-9-11.**
Who says God isn't alive? Some people pray for flashing signs. I got one that day!

While this was a sweet reminder for me personally, it also should bring hope to all of us! Why?

God has chosen ALL of us to give HOPE and SHINE in the darkness.
God has called ALL of us to STAND for His Word.
God has given ALL of us gifts we need to serve and minister for His glory.

But sometimes He has to knock us over the head with flashing signs to get His point across! God challenges ALL of us to KEEP on pedaling when we feel like giving up. Remember the sweet song at the beginning of this lesson —

"I still believe in the sun when there is no light
I still believe in the love when there is no one
I still believe in God."

Keep believing.
Keep remembering His promises.
AND . . . **D-on't Stop Pedaling.**

Lesson Three/ TENSION AND TIMING

Before we start today's lesson, let's review the positioning of the riders on the tandem as we continue to build our theme of D-on't Stop Pedaling.

"The captain is responsible for communicating with the stoker, calling out when to start pedaling, when to stop pedaling, when hazards or bumps are present in the road, when he is about to shift or brake, and any other information that the stoker needs to know. The stoker is responsible for listening to and following the captain's instructions without hesitation . . ."[2]

I love the last statement–**without hesitation.** Think about this for a minute. Do you follow God's lead without hesitation? Today, we are going to take a look at a very interesting component of the tandem called the **drive chain.** This is what Wikipedia says:

> "To transfer power from all pedals to the rear wheel requires a drive train. Typically, the forward crankset is connected by a left-side timing chain to the rear crankset, which in turn is connected by a right-side chain to the rear wheel."[3]

This is Annie's interpretation—The drive train is required to transfer power to the REAR tire where we are positioned. Because it is connected to the **timing** chain, the drive chain has to have the right amount of **tension** to transfer the force to the rear wheel.

Tension and timing. Sounds Biblical to me!

God uses tension in our lives to deepen our dependence on Him. If there was no tension, we would never experience His power. I believe many Christians seem to feel disconnected to the power when they can't explain the tension (i.e., the pain, the trouble, or the misunderstanding). When we can't see the road ahead or we can't understand why God is taking us through a difficult time, doubt sets in and we lose our focus. Instead of having more faith, we begin to doubt the Captain's capabilities and our thoughts become fixated on the anxieties of our day. Worry gets in the front seat and faith is left behind.

Let's read Psalm 22:1-3.

> "My God, my God, why have you forsaken me? Why are you so far from saving me, so far from my cries of anguish? My God, I cry out by day, but you do not answer, by night, but I find no rest. Yet you are enthroned as the Holy One; you are the one Israel praises. In you our ancestors put their trust; they trusted and you delivered them. To you they cried out and were saved; in you they trusted and were not put to shame." Psalm 22:1-3

> **At what point in these verses do you see the Psalmist shift focus? What do you think brought about this change?**

_____
_____
_____
_____
_____

Does the passage "My God, my God, why have you forsaken me?" ring a bell?

Read Matthew 27:46

This is what the Pulpit commentary says:

"Into the full meaning of this bitter cry we cannot venture irreverently to intrude. At the same time, thus much may be said. It was not mere bodily anguish that elicited it; it arose from some incalculable affliction of soul. He was bearing the sins of the whole world; the Lord had laid on him the iniquity of us all; there was no one to comfort him in his heaviness; and the light of God's countenance was for the time withdrawn from him. He was "left" that he might bear man's sins in their full and crushing weight, and by bearing save. . . . No answer came from the darkened heaven; but the cry was heard;

"About three in the afternoon Jesus cried out in a loud voice, "Eli, Eli, lema sabachthani?" (which means "My God, my God, why have you forsaken me?")
Matthew 27:46

the unspeakable sacrifice, a sacrifice necessary according to the Almighty's purpose, was accepted, and with his own blood he obtained eternal redemption for man."[4]

Tension and timing.

Love kept on pedaling. Love was A-ligned and took a N-ecessary Stop on this earth to rescue man from eternal separation from a Holy God. **Love never gave up.** Regardless of incalculable affliction of the soul, Jesus laid down his life for you and for me.

Love never gives up.

Read Hebrews 4:14-16.

Why do we hold firmly to our faith?

_____

_____

How can we identify with Jesus?

_____

_____

What is the basis upon which we can approach God's throne of grace with confidence?

_____

_____

What is promised?

_____

_____

In God's perfect timing, He sent His son to heal the broken relationship with mankind. By believing in the perfect life, death, and resurrection of His Son, Jesus Christ, we can now enter God's throne room and have a personal relationship with Jesus. We can cry out to Him and be saved. We can trust in Him and not be put to shame. This was impossible in the Old Testament. Connection with Jehovah only happened once a year when the high priest would enter the Holy of Holies to confess the sins of the people.

Today, we can approach the throne room because Jesus is our High Priest. We have 24-hour access. We can pray. We can read His Word. We can fellowship with other believers—ALL because **Jesus is the DRIVE TRAIN.** He is the connection that allows us to ride tandem with the God of the universe!

The reason there is power available beyond our circumstances is because **Jesus is the power source.** When you are face to face with a mountain of difficulty, are you going to tell God how big your mountain is OR are you going to tell your mountain how BIG your God is? I love what Tony Evans says, "Faith is in your FEET, not in your feelings."[5] How true. We tend to get so wrapped up in our feelings that we forget to focus on the power source. We need to switch the focus from our feelings to faith just like King David did in Psalm 22. Sure, he had his pity party in the beginning, but then we **see** the shift, the transformation when he remembers that God is enthroned. He is the Holy One. **He is the Captain.**

Read Romans 8:28.

What is the proof that tension and timing go hand in hand?

_____

_____

_____

```
There is purpose in the tension.
There is power in the timing.
```

I hope this lesson was as exciting for you as it was for me. In closing, I want to share with you a devotional from *Streams in the Desert* from April 9th. Keep in mind that in order to pedal forward, power is generated from the turning of the wheels and the tension of the drive train.

". . . when God desires to create more power in your life, He creates more friction. He uses this pressure to generate more spiritual power. Some people cannot handle it, and run from the pressure instead of receiving the power and using it to rise above the painful experience that produced it. Opposition is essential to maintaining the true balance between forces. . . . We are divinely propelled, let us press on with faith and patience in our high and heavenly calling."[6]
A. B. Simpson

Isn't it good to know that friction can be a good thing?

What in your life was produced by a painful result of friction? Can you enter the throne room with confidence and cry aloud to your Captain? Can you allow the pressure of any situation to generate spiritual power? One thing is for certain. You can't do this riding alone. **You need Jesus.** When He is the drive train, the connection of power to the back rider, we can switch our . . .

problems to **praise**,
troubles to **trust**,
worries to watching the **wonderful things**,
and fear to **freedom**.

My friend Susan New said this, "Our obstacles are not an end to us finding God, but rather a pathway to allow Him to take us to higher places."

Don't stop pedaling, my friend. There is perfect timing in the tension. Even if you feel, at times, disconnected to the power, Jesus is always steering you in the right direction. Lean into the power and trust in His leading. Amen!

Lesson Four/ GRACE TRAIN

```
I recently heard Crystal Evans Hurst candidly speak about her many
adventures riding bikes.
```

Naturally, when she started talking about bike riding, my ears perked up! With the same captivating story-telling talent as her father, Tony Evans, she told us about her many journeys riding over the Golden Gate Bridge. One journey was not so fortunate as she gained too much speed biking the downward slope into Sausalito. She admits the last thing she remembers is flying over her handlebars. After trying to convince herself she was just fine, her daughter pointed out the blood on her shirt and the alignment of her wrist. She was out of A-lignment and needed a N-ecessary Stop.

Many of us would have been bandaged up and given up. But not Crystal. She is one determined lady. She did not stop pedaling. She would later bike over the Golden Gate Bridge two more times. Learning from the lessons of her previous experiences, she allowed a painful experience to propel her forward to try again—in God's perfect tension and timing.

Today, I want to carry on the idea of **tension** and **timing** and look at two Biblical characters who allowed the pain in their lives to propel them toward Jesus. Let's read about Jairus and the bleeding woman in Luke chapter eight.

Read Luke 8:40-56.

In your own words, describe the setting of these verses.

_____

_____

What was the tension in this woman's life that led her to touch Jesus?

_____

_____

Consider the timing in this event. Where was Jesus headed when He felt the power go out of Him?

_____

_____

Why do you think this timing is significant?

_____

_____

What healed the bleeding woman?

_____

_____

What did Jesus tell Jairus about his daughter in verse 50? How would you have responded to this?

_____

_____

I find these two stories of Jesus' healing a beautiful picture of tension and timing merging into our chapter of D-on't Stop Pedaling. This is the question I ponder—What keeps us from pedaling? What keeps us from believing? For the following exercise, list as many barriers you can think of that would have stopped the bleeding woman and Jairus from pedaling toward the healing power of Jesus.

The Bleeding Woman:

_____

_____

_____

_____

Jairus:

_____

_____

_____

_____

_____

_____

_____

Now, it's your turn. Think of a problem or a tension in your life, either past or present, that keeps you from seeking Jesus. What stops you from reaching out to touch Him? What are your fears? What stops you from believing?

You:

_____

_____

_____

_____

_____

_____

_____

_____

I can name a few things that keep me from pedaling. Pride. Lack of time. Busyness. Unbelief. Getting other's advice first. Trusting in other's opinions. Thinking it will just go away if I ignore it. CONTROL. Wow. I don't know about you, but I just felt the Captain pull over the bike, spread out a blanket, and ask me to sit while He does some preaching into my soul!

Sometimes in life, we don't have it in us to take another step. Our circumstances are just too overwhelming. This is the exact time we need to let Jesus pedal for us. But so often, this is the exact time we leave our back seat and jump into central command. WE LOVE TO BE IN CONTROL. Why? We want to fix it fast. We want something we can see and touch. I love Casting Crown's new song because I can relate to the lyrics as a wife and a mom of four, leading a ministry, and trying my hardest to keep my house from not falling into disaster. It's called *Hold it All Together*.[7]

> Everybody needs you strong
> But life hits you out of nowhere
> And barely leaves you holding on
>
> And when you're tired of fighting
> Chained by your control
> There's freedom in surrender
> Lay it down and let it go
>
> So when you're on your knees and answers seem so far away
> You're not alone, stop holding on and just be held
> Your world's not falling apart, its falling into place
> I'm on the throne, stop holding on and just be held
> Just be held, just be held

What line gets your attention? For me it was "Chained by your control." To think I hold my life together is a joke. It's not reality. God is holding me, and He is holding you. He is steadying the bike so we can hop on and be aligned with Him. He wants us to trust in His leading and perfect timing. He wants us to believe and not fear what's ahead. He wants us to lean into His direction—even when life seems to be falling apart. Who do we turn to when we are overwhelmed? Do we reach out and touch Jesus? Do we stop Him amidst our crowded day? When we **identify the tension**, we will **see** where we need to drop the chains of control.

While tension can certainly drive us away from Jesus, it can also **propel us to pedal forward and believe in His power.** The stories of the bleeding woman and Jairus reveal to us that Jesus will stop at any moment in time, listen to our sorrows, and repair the chain. There is no judgement or condemnation. He's available and accessible. Twenty-four hours a day.

As we close for today, notice where Jesus was headed in the story. He was on the way to heal a dying child. That's urgent, right? If you were Jesus' disciple and the ruler of the synagogue came and requested your presence, my guess is that you would get there pronto! But not Jesus. He gives His listening ear to ALL His beloved children, whether they are a high-class official or a low-class bleeding woman. He, like His Father, does not show favoritism. In His perfect timing, Jesus had TIME to stop and listen to the story of this bleeding woman. I imagine after 12 years of bleeding, her story lasted as least 15 minutes. We will never know for sure. What we do know is that Jesus' N-ecessary Stop was long enough for Jairus' daughter to die. But, in His perfect tension and timing, he heals Jairus' daughter and brings her back to life.

The lesson here is that Jesus has TIME for each of our tensions. When we keep pedaling toward Him, there is a power that helps us believe the impossible. We are not promised instant healing, but we are filled with **hope.** When we are up against ALL that convinces us to stop believing, I encourage you to keep pedaling. Rely on the leading of the Captain to provide the power as He pedals **with you.** This is the beauty of a tandem bike.

Keep your feet on the pedals, don't be afraid, and believe His power is propelling you forward.

In closing, read the following verses. What do these verses tell us about God's love for us?

- **1 Corinthians 13:7**

"Love never gives up, never loses faith, is always hopeful and endures through every circumstance." 1 Corinthians 13:7 (NLT)

_____
_____
_____
_____
_____

- **Ephesians 2:4-5**

_____
_____
_____
_____
_____

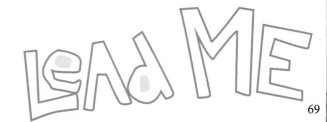

We are alive, my friend. It's not that we were bad and then made good because of Jesus. We were once dead and are now made **ALIVE** through Jesus. Looking back into these stories of surrender, belief, trust, and love, it's really not the drive train that connects the power to the back rider. **It's the grace train.** It is because of His great love for us. It is this very connection to Christ that gives us the power to overcome and be overwhelmed by His love and peace. Jesus doesn't have grease on His hands when He stops to realign our chain. No. These are blood-stained hands. They are filled with grace to love us during our hardest days and deepest doubts. Do you trust in your Captain to lead you? When you feel like giving up, lean in to the leading of the Commander in Chief. He has the connections! Amen.

If you are struggling with control, write a prayer using what we have learned today.

_____

_____

_____

_____

_____

_____

_____

Lesson Five/ THE BOOM

We started off week four with the word "lead." Let's end with this idea as well.

Begin by reading Psalm 78:70-72.

Who chose David as his servant?

_____

_____

What was his job before he was chosen as King?

_____

_____

How many times do you see the word sheep or shepherd in these verses?

_____

_____

How did he lead the people?

_____

_____

God chose David to lead the people of Israel, and He took him from shepherding sheep to shepherding people. I love this transition. Don't pass by it too quickly. Four times in three verses, the 78th Psalm reminds us that God took David from the sheep pens to being the shepherd over Israel. I bet David never thought he could use his youthful days of protecting sheep to protecting God's children as the King of Israel. Think about this. God can use **any gift** you have for His Kingdom. I believe God uses my gifts of creativity to write and design Bible studies. I believe God uses my husband's gifts of law to research the Scriptures and lead an amazing Sunday School class. I believe God uses my daughter's gifts of organization to lead the vestry at her high school.

What skills has God given you to use for His Kingdom?

_____

_____

_____

_____

I love that the Bible tells us "with skillful hands he led them." Simple, yet powerful. One thing we know about sheep is that they are not very smart. They are always hungry and thirsty, and they get scared quickly. They are totally dependent on the shepherd for protection, care, food, and health. With skillful hands, the shepherd has to look ahead for potential danger, lead the flock to green pasture, still the waters so they can drink, heal their wounds, seek those that are lost, and find the ones who have strayed. I imagine there are a lot of sleepless nights and many prayers for patience and love. The words shepherds, sheep, and shepherding are used more than 250 times in the Bible. There is a reason, because there is a **connection.**

Jesus is our Good Shepherd. With skillful hands, HE LEADS us. **It's a beautiful picture.** Think of ALL the things His hands have created.

Colossians 1:16 tells us this:

"For by him all things were created: things in heaven and on earth, visible and invisible, whether thrones or powers or rulers or authorities; all things were created by him and for him." Colossians 1:16

Look up the following verses and list ALL the wonders He has created.

   • **Acts 17:24**

   _____

   _____

   • **Psalm 19:1**

   _____

   _____

   • **Psalm 8:3**

   "When I consider your heavens, the work of your fingers, the moon and the stars, which you have set in place . . . " Psalm 8:3

   _____

   _____

   • **Genesis 1:1, Genesis 1:20-21, 24, Genesis 1:27**

   _____

   _____

   • **Psalm 139:13-14**

   _____

   _____

With skillful hands, God created everything.
With skillful hands,
God made YOU.

I believe sometimes we stop pedaling because we don't think we have anything to offer. That's baloney. You have been created by God. You are not an accident. God knit you with **purpose.** He gave you gifts and talents so you can use them to **lead** others to Him. With skillful hands, **God made you.** And He will **lead** you.

Let's pick up on the verse we started reading yesterday.

Read Ephesians 2:4-10.

How have we been saved?

_____

_____

Why can we not save ourselves?

_____

_____

What does God call us?

_____

_____

It's important to KNOW we were made alive in Christ by grace before we can jump to the amazing reality that we are God's workmanship. Sometimes we can think we are more superior than we really are. Remember, we are lost sheep! But unlike sheep, we are created in Christ Jesus to do good works, which God prepared in advance for us to do. Again, you are no mistake. God created you KNOWING in advance that only YOU would have the certain gifts and talents you could use to bring Him glory, just like David. Pretty cool.

Curry and I were on an anniversary trip when we met a delightful couple from Darien, Connecticut. We soon learned they were very proud grandparents and even more proud of the names their grandchildren had given them. I think the naming of your own child is hard. I imagine the grandparent naming ceremony must be a right of passage. Enough of the suspense. What was the grandfather's name? **Boom.** Yep. That's right. He was a larger man and when his grandchildren would run up to give him a big hug, they would always yell, "Boom!" The naming conundrum was solved.

`Boom it was.`

I like to think of God as my BOOM. When I run and jump into His arms, I sense the connection, the surrender, the letting go of my control, and feel the BOOM. Like a child being fully enveloped in the arms of a HUGE hug, I want this freedom to be loved unconditionally. I just want to let go and believe with unabandoned passion that He is leading me with skillful hands. The hands that formed the heavens and earth are holding me. The hands that announced the stars and gave the light to the sky gave me my passions and gifts. The hands that call in powers and authorities, call me to serve with integrity of heart. These hands made me with a plan and a purpose. BOOM

If you are like me, sometimes you want to give up, grab the steering wheel of control, and stop pedaling altogether. Here is a **BOOM prayer** for those moments. Let's pray it together.

Dear Lord, I am a child of God, an original masterpiece. I am chosen, forgiven, and loved by the Prince of Peace. I have gifts and talents that You want me to use to lead others to You. I am a new creation. By your love, I am righteous and redeemed. I am saved by Your love and grace alone. I am worthy and more than enough. I am called to live out my gifts and serve one another. I am loved.

You are the Boom. I am the beloved. Ride on. Amen.

We are going to be looking at THREE ways to pedal.

    1. Pedaling in our _____ power.
    2. Pedaling in the _____ power.
    3. Pedaling with _____ power.

1. Pedaling in our own power.

• When we are not awake, we will fall _____ to the things of God.
• The Spirit is willing, but the _____ is weak.

2. Pedaling in the Spirit's power.

• With Jesus as your Captain, you can do ALL things through Him who strengthens you.

3. Pedaling with enough power.

• We keep on pedaling because Jesus said, "_____."

"My soul is overwhelmed with sorrow to the point of death," he said to them. "Stay here and keep watch." Going a little farther, he fell to the ground and prayed that if possible the hour might pass from him. "Abba, Father," he said, "everything is possible for you. Take this cup from me. Yet not what I will, but what you will."

Mark 14:34-36 (NIV)

Answers: own, Spirit's, enough, asleep, flesh, enough

Week FIVE: Lesson One/ ENJOY THE RIDE

Week five is about E-njoying the Ride. Boy, do I need to be reminded of this truth!

I love that while I am writing this Bible study, God is teaching me volumes about Riding Tandem with Him. E-njoying the Ride is about maintaining a JOY-filled spirit as we ride with God in this tandem journey. This week we will discover how our fruit allows us to enJOY the present moment—even when life is not going the direction we intend. E-njoying the Ride will take complete surrender and trust as we follow the leader, especially when our lives seem to be racing at ninety miles to nothing. We will learn that a key to E-njoying the Ride is to have a heart of praise. We will also learn that laughter is a good thing! Our Captain is creative and not always serious. He offers hope and is the provider of **all** our enjoyment. E-njoying the Ride is essential to our tandem journey. Let's get started!

We are going to start our week by reading Numbers 14:1-8.

To give you some background, we see the Israelites complaining **again** that their days in Egypt were more glorious than their current situation in the desert (Numbers 14:1-4). We have already learned that a complaining heart tends to exaggerate our circumstances, but here we see it can also steal our joy. In the previous chapter (Numbers 13), Joshua, Caleb, and 10 other men were sent on a mission to spy out the promised land that God had given them. Their job was to investigate. What kind of land was it? Who lived there? What kind of soil did it have? What about the trees? When they returned, they gave a great report on the land. They even brought back a sample of the fruit. But while Caleb and Joshua were gung-ho to take possession of the promised land, the other men spread a bad report that the people were too gigantic to conquer. Fear struck and the Israelites were paralyzed.

Read Numbers 14:1-9.

Describe the fear of the people going into the promised land. (Numbers 14:3)

_____

_____

How do Caleb and Joshua try to convince the people that going is good?

_____

_____

_____

What is the Lord's promise to the Israelites if they choose to follow His lead?

_____

_____

_____

What is Joshua and Caleb's warning to the people? (Numbers 14:9)

_____

_____

_____

Why are we studying this passage on our first day of E-njoying the Ride? In order to experience the JOY of the Lord in the present moment, we have to FIRST learn to **follow** where He leads. We cannot rebel and do our own thing. We cannot allow the fear of our circumstances to override the confidence in our Captain. We cannot let what we **see** (or think we see) steal our joy and our assurance that God is our leader. He is WITH us. Caleb and Joshua were sent ahead to scout out the land, and they came back with fruit. GOOD fruit—solid proof that the land they were to conquer was a **future blessing**. At this point, the Israelite's diet was manna and quail. I would have enjoyed a little fruit, too, wouldn't you?

For a fun exercise, let's look at what fruit represents in Scripture.

Look up the following verses. Identify the fruit and share how good fruit will allow you to E-njoy the Ride.

- **Psalm 128:1-4**

  _____
  _____
  _____

- **Galatians 5:22-23**

  _____
  _____
  _____

> "Blessed are all who fear the Lord, who walk in His ways. You will eat the fruit of your labor; blessings and prosperity will be yours."
>
> Psalm 128:1-4

- **Proverbs 12:14**

  _____
  _____

- **Proverbs 11:30**

  _____
  _____

- **Hosea 10:12**

  "I said, 'Plant the good seeds of righteousness, and you will harvest a crop of love. Plow up the hard ground of your hearts, for now is the time to seek the LORD, that he may come and shower righteousness upon you.'" Hosea 10:12 (NLT)

  _____
  _____

Our fruit can be our attitude, our words, our work, our actions, our praise, our worship, and our thanksgiving. Our fruit represents what is in our heart, and what is **in** our heart can come **out** of our mouths at any unexpected moment.

I was at little Curry's varsity football game on a recent Friday night. I did not realize that every time the opposing team scored a touchdown, a cannon fired off. A LOUD cannon. I was purchasing my ticket when the blast almost scared Jesus right out of me. I screamed, "GOOD LORD!" right into the ears of a police officer standing next to me. I looked at her and with laughter said, "I sure am thankful THAT came out!" Who knows what could have come out of my mouth in that split second? Let's give a shout out to some good fruit! When we eat good fruit, **goodness comes out.**

Read Matthew 12:33-35.

"A tree is identified by its fruit. If a tree is good, its fruit will be good. If a tree is bad, its fruit will be bad. You brood of snakes! How could evil men like you speak what is good and right? For whatever is in your heart determines what you say. A good person produces good things from the treasury of a good heart, and an evil person produces evil things from the treasury of an evil heart."

To be able to E-njoy the Ride, good fruit must be in our hearts. Fruit can go either way. It can be fresh or as rotten as the bad influence of the unbelieving spies. Because of their fear, the Israelites ignored Caleb and Joshua's report and even wanted to stone Moses and Aaron and initiate new leadership. Lesson to learn: We will follow the wrong leader when we have bad fruit in our hearts. When we sow the promises of Scripture into our hearts, we can E-njoy the Ride because we are confident that our Captain is with us. He is leading us into good land even when there is fear or uncertainty. You cannot E-njoy the Ride when there is bad fruit spoiling the basket of your circumstance. Don't allow the appearance of your surroundings to scare you from the promises of God. The fruit from the Promise Land is always good.

Today, live in this truth. E-njoy the Ride because the **fruit of Scripture is good!** Shout it out when the circumstances of life are weighing you down. Shout it out when you are afraid of what the future might hold. Shout it out when others are trying to convince you that God is not real. Shout it out—especially at ballgames when loud cannons are trying to scare Jesus right out of you! Shout it out. Good Lord! **He is good.**

Lesson Two/ COWBOY CAVIAR

Last fall, I was invited by a group of girls to a beautiful home in South Carolina for a little R and R. One of the best parts about the weekend was that ALL the plans had been made.

My friend Courtney, who coordinated the trip, had the driving directions printed, a schedule of events planned, dinner reservations made in advance, and even met us at the front door with Cowboy Caviar (recipe included at end of this chapter!). Because I was following the car ahead of me, I did not have to navigate the road ahead. I drove up and down the hills of South Carolina without a care in the world listening to awesome Christian music and mesmerized that leaves do change color north of Florida! I was E-njoying the Ride. Ahhhhh. The sweet memories.

What do the following verses say about how we are to plan our steps?

• **Proverbs 16:9**

_____

• **Proverbs 19:21**

_____

_____

• **Psalm 37:23-24**

_____

_____

The word for *establish* in Proverbs 16:9 and *makes firm* in Psalm 37:23 is *kuwn* which means to set up, to be firm, to be established, be prepared.[1] The word for *prevails* in Proverbs 19:21 is *quwm* which also means to establish, to stand, to set.[2] It is clear to me that God's **purpose** for our lives is **purpose-full.** We are not a cosmic mistake. God did not haphazardly make you one day on His lunch break. No! God set your plans into motion and established them with purpose. When bumps hit here and there, they do not take God by surprise. We can learn to E-njoy the Ride during the good times and the bad times by holding on and LEANING into the One who is LEADING. Read what Mark Batterson says in *Draw the Circle, The 40-Day Prayer Challenge.*

"God wants us to get where God wants us to go more than we want to get where God wants us to go. Follow the script of the Holy Scripture and the Improvisation of the Holy Spirit."[3]

You might have to read that again. Slowly. It's too good to miss. I love this quote because it reminds me of my childhood modern dance teacher, Diann Catlin. As a warm-up for class, she would have us dance "improvisations." She would tell us to dance like we are a piece of gum stuck to the bottom of a shoe or a car shifting gears or a hurricane or a flower opening or a kitchen disposal. You name it, we probably danced it. I loved improvisations! Here we are reminded that God has already established our steps. We are called to imitate Him and dance with abandon to the tune of the Holy Spirit.

What do these verses tell us about Scripture and following the Holy Spirit?

- **Deuteronomy 5:1**

_____

_____

- **Exodus 18:20**

_____

_____

_____

- **Psalm 143:8**

"Let the morning bring me word of your unfailing love, for I have put my trust in you. Show me the way I should go, for to you I entrust my life." Psalm 143:8

_____

_____

_____

- **Psalm 32:8**

_____

_____

_____

- **Ephesians 5:1-2**

_____

_____

_____

"Therefore be imitators of God, as beloved children. And walk in love, as Christ loved us and gave himself up for us, a fragrant offering and sacrifice to God."

Ephesians 5:1-2

Learning Scripture is like learning the choreography to a beautiful dance. We are to imitate the moves of the Teacher and watch the way He dances. This takes time and discipline. We can't just step out on the stage of life without knowing, learning, listening to, and watching the Master Choreographer. We have to **practice** so that when we are called to dance, we know the steps. In ballet, we are told to dance "full-out." I think this can apply to our lives, as well.

Because we have placed full trust in the choreography, we can dance FULL OUT and E-njoy the Ride. We don't even have to worry about forgetting the steps as long as we are following the script of the Scriptures. The Holy Spirit will remind us of the steps just when we need them. Your dance is choreographed with an established purpose and inspired with passion and love. Without further a-do, I believe the curtain is rising. Its your turn to take the stage and dance. Enjoy the ride (and the Cowboy Caviar!).

Dear Jesus, thank You for being our Master Choreographer! You have established our steps with purpose. You have gone before us to prepare the way so that we don't have to worry about what is ahead. You are in charge of the choreography. Our job is to learn the steps of Scripture so we can dance FULL-OUT with passion and love. I pray our dance would inspire and touch the lives of others so they, too, will want to know the Maker of our dance. Amen.

COWBOY CAVIAR Recipe:

INGREDIENTS
2 (14-ounce) cans Black-Eyed Peas (unseasoned and drained)
2 (14-ounce) can White Shoepeg Corn (drained)
8 Roma Tomatoes (chopped fine, no seeds) or 3 Regular Tomatoes
1 medium red, orange or yellow Bell Pepper
1 bunch of Green Onions (chopped fine)
1 bunch of Cilantro (chopped fine)
1 to 2 Jalapeños, ribs removed, seeded and finely chopped
1 Avocado (optional)
1 bottle of Newman's Own Family recipe Italian dressing (1/2 to 1/3 of bottle)
1 package of Feta Cheese (use best judgement on amount)

INSTRUCTIONS :
In a large serving bowl, combine the drained black-eyed peas, corn, chopped tomatoes, bell pepper, onion, cilantro and jalapeño. If you'll be including avocado, wait to dice it until you're ready to serve the dip, so it doesn't turn brown in the meantime. Drizzle the dressing over the serving bowl and toss until well mixed. For best flavor, let the mixture marinate for at least 20 minutes before serving. If you're adding avocado, mix it in just before serving. Serve with Frito Lay Big Scoop Corn Chips and your favorite friends!

Lesson Three/ SURRENDER

When I sit down and think about E-njoying this tandem Ride with God, why is it that my mind tends to go to the things I have "to-do" or better yet, haven't done? Are you are like me?

Does your "to-do" list and "haven't-done" list wake you up in the morning before you get coffee? Life seems to take over and go by at such a fast pace that it doesn't seem possible to stop and E-njoy the Ride. How do we do this? How do we enjoy this tandem ride with God while our lives are so busy? We have seen how mountainous obstacles can steal our joy and our fruit. We have also learned how Scripture guides us to dance the steps God has established and planned out for us. But, honestly, how do we E-njoy the Ride? For the next three lessons, we will look at three ways: **surrender**, **praise**, and **tandem stories**.

Today, we are going to look at **surrender.** At first, this word might not look like a fun tandem bike experience, but I promise, it will be the best ride you will ever take!

Read Joshua 3:1-17.

What does God tell the people to do today to prepare for tomorrow? Why do you think this would be significant in our tandem journey with God?

_____
_____
_____
_____
_____
_____

The word for sanctify can mean to purify, to be set apart, to consecrate.[4] Google tells us that the word for consecrate means to dedicate formally to a divine purpose. What I hear God telling us is this: You cannot be about your own purposes and God's promises at the same time. You need to surrender your agenda because it competes with God's agenda. It is like oil and water. I hear God saying loud and clear that in order to E-njoy the Ride, we need to SURRENDER our control! Ladies, this means no hands on the handlebars! Check out the promise in Joshua 3:5. If we sanctify, or set apart our lives, and learn the choreography of Scripture **today,** then **tomorrow** we will see the wonders of God! The word for wonder is the same word for wonderful used in Psalm 119:18.

> "And Joshua said unto the people, **sanctify** yourselves: for tomorrow the LORD will do **wonders** among you."
>
> Joshua 3:5 (KJV)

"Open my eyes that I may see wonderful things in your law." Psalm 119:18

Do you remember what wonderful means? It is the things that we, in and of ourselves, cannot do on our own. It is the surpassing, marvelous, beyond's one power, and too difficult to understand things. God will show Himself wonderful if we consecrate ourselves today.

This passage in Joshua describes the **wonderful things** God was about to do for the people of Israel. They had served their sentence in the desert for 40 years and now God was giving them a second chance to enter the promised land through the leadership of Joshua. This time they were not scared of giants. They did not retreat back into their own plans. Instead, they were COMPLETELY SURRENDERED to step into the Jordan at flood stage. As soon as their feet touched the water, the river dried up and they were able to cross on dry land! I call that a WONDER—a miracle that only God could have done. The Israelites fully surrendered their lives into the promises of God and were about **to dance** into the promised land.

You cannot be about your own purposes and God's promises at the same time.

LEAD ME

What do the following verses tell us about how God's faithfulness will never leave us as we dance into His promises?

• **Isaiah 52:12**

"You will not leave in a hurry, running for your lives. For the LORD will go ahead of you; yes, the God of Israel will protect you from behind." Isaiah 52:12 (NLT)

_____

_____

_____

• **Exodus 13:21**

_____

_____

_____

• **Exodus 14:13**

_____

_____

_____

I have friends who don't want to believe in Jesus because they feel they will lose their independence. They associate losing control with trusting in Jesus. Nothing could be further from the truth. The more we grip onto the "I'm-going-to-do-this-my-way" attitude, the further we backtrack into the desert and away from the promised land. In order to E-njoy the Ride, we have to stop trying to steer the handlebars from the back. They don't move, and they will never steer no matter how hard we try. Remember lesson four in N-ecessary Stops? By taking the first small steps of faith to believe, our eyes will be open to see the wonderful things of God. We have to **believe first** in order for us to **see** the promises of God. The verses above are a fresh reminder that God goes ahead of us and guides us. We do not have to be afraid. We don't have to be awakened by our "to-do" lists and jump out of bed to speed into our day. Did you catch what Exodus 14:13 tells us to do in order to E-njoy the Ride? We have to **stand still.** We have to be still in order to WATCH God in our lives.

Take a look at these two words: STAND and STILL. How do you think the strength of these words together will allow you to E-njoy the Ride? Why not just stand? Why not just be still? Why is there more power when they ride tandem together?

_____

_____

_____

_____

_____

_____

_____

_____

_____

_____

In order for us to E-njoy the Ride, we have to STAND on the foundation of Scripture and sit STILL while God directs our purposeful paths. As much as we want to be in control, we need to fully consecrate and surrender to the ride. Trust Him, let go of the back handlebars, and feel the breeze!

If you think you are losing the race by taking the time to sit still, I am here to encourage you today! You are actually winning the race because you are surrendering your agenda to the God who has your life in the palm of His hand. Read this excerpt from the poem, *Sit Still*.

"Sit still, my daughter, just sit calmly still. What higher service could you for Him fill? It's hard! Ah, yes! But choicest things must cost! For lack of losing and how much is lost! It's hard, it's true! But then—He gives you grace to count the hardest spot the sweetest place." J. Danson Smith [5]

In closing, write down the specific things you are going to surrender today to the One who knows how hard it is to give up control. Even Jesus let His Father have the front seat. He died on the cross for you and for me. Because He did, we can E-njoy the Ride. Because of His SURRENDER, we can SEE the wonderful things the Lord has for us. Consecrate yourselves and sit still today so you can WATCH for all the amazing things God will do tomorrow!

_____
_____
_____
_____
_____
_____
_____
_____
_____
_____
_____
_____
_____
_____
_____
_____

Lesson Four PRAISE

I hope you feel a little lighter this morning as you surrender control over to the One who is steering your tandem journey!

I can't wait to see what God will show you in your life today because you surrendered yesterday! Keep watch! Keep your eyes OPEN and look for the mighty hand of God.

Today, we are going to look at how PRAISE allows us to E-njoy the Ride! Instead of looking at all the things that are going wrong, let's praise God for all that is **going right!** I love this prayer I wrote in my journal. I hope it will encourage you, too!

Today Lord, I choose to hop on the back seat of the tandem and let You steer. Where are You taking me today? Yes, I will pedal, and yes, I will trust. While I can't see the road ahead, I believe You can. You have gone before me and because I have spent time in Your Word, I am prepared to ride with You today. I am equipped because You are my lead and my guide. There may be times when I am afraid and clutch a little too tightly to my handlebars, but I know You will never leave Your seat as the Captain of my life. I may want You to pedal faster to speed things up. I may ask You to slow things down, or perhaps stop, so I can catch my breath. I know You've got this Lord, and You have my best interest in Your heart. We are a team as we ride tandem together. With You as my Captain, we will win this race. We will press on together until the finish line. Steady my bike, sweet Lord, so that I may climb on. Balance the bike for me so I can take my position on the back. I am Your co-captain. Lead me into the way everlasting. Amen.

Today, let's celebrate the ride of our LIVES and give the Captain some **praise**. He's got this. It does not matter how big or little your circumstances, He knows the road ahead. Let's not look at what's going wrong, but rather shift our eyes on ALL that's going **right.** Today, focus on ALL that He has done for YOU and shout out some PRAISE!

Look up the following verses and write down all the reasons you can E-njoy the Ride!

> • **Psalm 118:24**
>
> "This is the day that the LORD has made; let us rejoice and be glad in it." Psalm 118:24
>
> _____
> _____
> _____

> • **Psalm 95:1-7**
>
> _____
> _____
> _____
> _____
> _____

> • **Proverbs 31:25**
>
> _____
> _____
> _____
> _____

> • **Psalm 65:1-8**
>
> _____
> _____
> _____
> _____
> _____

These are just a few verses that give us a reason to E-njoy the Ride! Our God is simply amazing. I know that when my life feels overwhelming, I seem to forget who God is. I need to shout out some PRAISE instead of focusing on my problems. Come, let us sing for JOY to the Lord! He has created **everything** we look at **every day.** That alone should get our hearts excited to rejoice! We are to PRAISE the One who gave us laughter. Don't take life too seriously. We CAN laugh at the days to come when we are seated in the back trusting in the Captain. Why is it that I tend to focus on Christ's sufferings so much. What about ALL His creativity, fun, and LAUGHTER? You just know the disciples laughed when they saw the fish had coins in his mouth. Wait . . . what?

Read Matthew 17:24-27.

> **What happens in this story that is super creative. How can we rejoice in Jesus' fun side?**
>
> _____
> _____
> _____
> _____

The point of reading this story is not to decide who is or who is not exempt from paying the king's taxes. What I want you to notice is how creative and FUN Jesus is! He could have paid this tax in so many ways. But He decided to use a fish with the exact money in his mouth to teach His disciples to trust Him in ALL things. How WONDERful is this lesson!

I asked you yesterday to write down the things you were going to surrender to God in order for Him to show you His wonders. Today, I want you to write down the WONDERS that God has shown you. Once you have written the wonders, write a PRAISE next to them. The ride is getting exciting! Doesn't it feel good to rejoice? 🚲

Wonders	Praise
_____/	_____
_____/	_____
_____/	_____
_____/	_____
_____/	_____
_____/	_____
_____/	_____
_____/	_____

Let's end today with Psalm 100—a Psalm of thanksgiving using the God's Word translation.

> "Shout happily to the LORD, all the earth. Serve the LORD cheerfully. Come into his presence with a joyful song. Realize that the LORD alone is God. He made us, and we are his. We are his people and the sheep in his care. Enter his gates with a song of thanksgiving. Come into his courtyards with a song of praise. Give thanks to him; praise his name. The LORD is good. His mercy endures forever. His faithfulness endures throughout every generation." Psalm 100 (GW)

To E-njoy this Ride, we must rejoice! When you greet God in the morning, shout out His name and THANK Him for all the goodness in your life. Why? Because He is GOOD, and His love endures forever. And ever. And ever. Forevermore. Have you ever noticed the **more** on forever? That is a LONG bike ride, my friend! Let's learn to E-njoy the Ride on this side of the abundant life that Christ offers.

Lesson Five/ TANDEM STORIES

It's our last day in E-njoy the Ride.

I hope you have discovered that we need to worry less and praise more! I want to start out today by reading a quote from Sarah Young in *Jesus Calling.*

> "Learn to enjoy life more. Relax. Remembering that I am God with you. I crafted you with enormous capacity to know Me and to ENJOY my presence."[6]

One of the ways I believe God crafts us with the capacity to KNOW Him is by **using our stories to tandem with the truths of Scripture.** As a speaker, I have always been taught to weave in personal stories to make God's Word more applicable. This truth is not only for speakers, but also for everyone of us. If you think about it, the entire Bible contains stories of men and women whose lives were touched by the truth of Scripture. In order to E-njoy this Ride, we need to weave our stories into Scripture and tell others of God's amazing grace! When we understand the Bible in a more personal way, I believe God becomes real. E-njoying the Ride is allowing God to use our stories to teach us the truth of His Word.

This past summer, Daley and her friend, Adam, were hiking in the Smoky Mountains. When they got to the top of their hike, they decided to take a path down that was not well traveled. About an hour into the trip, they were **lost.** With little cell phone reception, Adam managed to call his Mom, Kellie. Adam told her the situation, but couldn't tell her their location. When Kellie got to the parking lot to hike up the mountain to find them, she ran into a couple that was about to hike up this exact trail. She told them her concern and without hesitation the man went to his trunk, grabbed his hiking vest, three water bottles, a compass, a knife (to bushwhack if necessary), and took off.

Kellie was a little stunned and asked his wife if this was a normal response. "Yes," she responded. "He is a retired Navy Seal. It's what he does. It's how he **serves. He will find them.**" When the kind woman exchanged phone numbers with Kellie, the man's wife had to open her phone with a password. Do you know what it was? TRUST IN GOD. Amazing, right?

This story not only allowed me to trust God more, but it also showed Kellie, Daley and Adam to **trust more**, too! God showed Himself in a very real and tangible way that day. Let's take this story and look at one in Scripture that might resonate in our hearts the same way.

Let's read Luke 15:1-7.

> **What did the shepherd do when he learned one of his sheep was missing? How did the shepherd celebrate when he found the lost sheep?**

> _____

> _____

> **How does Jesus use this story to parallel the truth that all heaven celebrates when one lost soul is found?**

> _____

> _____

> _____

"And when he finds it, he joyfully puts it on his shoulders and goes home. Then he calls his friends and neighbors together and says, 'Rejoice with me; I have found my lost sheep.'"

Luke 15:5-6

When Daley told me the story of how they were lost and then found, **I celebrated!** When I learned that a retired Navy Seal left his wife and Kellie in the parking lot to hike up the mountain to find Daley and Adam, my mind triggered the story of the lost sheep. Mr. Navy Seal, just like the shepherd, was not going to stop until they were found. Jesus didn't stop either. **It's who He is. It's how He serves.** He sacrificed everything so that we could be found and saved. He sacrificed His life so we could make it to the party of salvation and eternal life. That's a day of rejoicing!

Why should we E-njoy the Ride? Because there is a lot of **rejoicing** to be done!

Look at the following verses. Find the word ENJOY and write down why we should be joyful.

• **Deuteronomy 6:1-2**

_____

_____

_____

_____

_____

• **Psalm 37:3-4**

_____

_____

_____

_____

• **Ephesians 6:1-3**

_____

_____

_____

_____

• **1 Timothy 6:17**

_____

_____

_____

_____

_____

We get to ENJOY a long life when we follow the ways of the Lord. When we TRUST in Him and do good, we will ENJOY safe pasture. When we obey our parents, we will ENJOY a long life on this earth (I use this one a lot!). We need to put our hope in God and not in wealth, which is so uncertain, because God is the only ONE who can provide for our true enJOYment. I love how the New Living Translation reads:

"Teach those who are rich in this world not to be proud and not to trust in their money, which is so unreliable. Their trust should be in God, who richly gives us all we need for our enjoyment."
1 Timothy 6:17

Did you catch that? I have been saving this verse for last because this is the very reason we can E-njoy the Ride! GOD is the ONLY ONE who can provide the enJOYment! If this statement is true, and I wholeheartedly believe it is, then why do we not enjoy **all** that God has provided? I think it is because we focus on what we don't have and miss out on what we DO HAVE. What a joy killer.

I find myself in this place too often. How about you? Put on the brakes. Stop the bike. Look at your positioning. Chances are, my friend, you are in the wrong seat and dancing to the wrong song. Your fruit has become sour, and you are not completely surrendered to the direction of your Captain. Climb on the back and lean into the leading of God. He has given you **everything you need.** Relax and remember His goodness.

As we close for the week, write down all the things God has placed in your life for you to E-njoy the Ride. Be creative. This is a FUN ride!

_____

_____

_____

_____

_____

_____

_____

_____

_____

_____

_____

_____

_____

_____

_____

_____

_____

_____

_____

_____

_____

_____

_____

_____

_____

_____

_____

_____

_____

_____

_____

_____

_____

_____

_____

_____

_____

_____

WOW. What a week! I hope you needed another piece of paper to write down all that God has given you to enjoy this incredible life. No mountain is too high and no valley is too deep for God to pour out His love on His children. God is always with us and will never leave us. As we close with prayer, remember that our Lord richly gives us all that we NEED for us to E-njoy the Ride. Great job.

Thank you Lord, for all You have shown us this week about E-njoying the Ride. We have so much to be thankful for. Teach us to trust in You no matter the enormity of our circumstance. Please do not allow the fear of the unknown to override our confidence in You. You have made us with purpose as we dance to Your choreography. Help us to surrender today so we can SEE Your wonders tomorrow. We need to stand still to fulfill the purposes You have set before us. May we always rejoice and praise You for all we have been given. Thank You that You never give up on us, but keep looking for us when we lose our way. Continue to use our stories to deepen our relationship with You. Help us to show others how amazing You are. I pray we would E-njoy this tandem ride because only You can fulfill our heart's deepest desires. Only with You can we E-njoy this Ride. Lead us, Lord, and teach us to lean into Your leading. Amen.

There are THREE simple ways we can E-njoy the Ride.

    1. Fill up with _____.

    2. _____ will guard your heart and mind.

    3. Putting your faith into _____.

1. Fill up with PRAISE! Rejoice in the Lord!

• EN is a prefix meaning in the state of something. To EN-JOY means we are in the condition or state of _____.

• The direct object of rejoice is — "Rejoice in the _____."

2. Peace will guard your heart and mind in Christ Jesus.

> "Rejoice in the Lord always. I will say it again: Rejoice! Let your gentleness be evident to all. The Lord is near. Do not be anxious about anything, but in every situation, by prayer and petition, with thanksgiving, present your requests to God. And the peace of God, which transcends all understanding, will guard your hearts and your minds in Christ Jesus.
>
> Philippians 4:4-7 (NIV)

3. Put your faith into PRACTICE.

• To Enjoy the Ride, we need to ask the Lord, "What _____ I do?"

Answers: praise, peace, practice, joy, Lord, can

Week SIX: Lesson One/ MARK THE MOMENTS

We did it! We are in the final week of Riding Tandem, and it's time to M-ark the Moments. However, this will not be our last stop.

Riding Tandem with the Lord means that we get to ride on, and on, and on . . . until the promised finish line where we will see Jesus face to face. Remember, this ride is only the beginning. **Eternity is forever.** This is the **hope** that allows us to M-ark the Moment. Any moment.

As a refresher, lets look again at Riding T. A. N. D. E. M. Let's begin with T-ime for Takeoff and the importance of A-ligning ourselves with the direction of our Captain.

> **T-ime for Takeoff**
> **A-lignment**

Let's review Psalm 139:23-24.

"Search me, God, and know my heart; test me and know my anxious thoughts. See if there is any offensive way in me, and lead me in the way everlasting." Psalm 139:23-24

Why would these verses be important for T-ime for Takeoff? What about A-lignment?

_____

_____

_____

_____

_____

Before we ride with God in the morning (T-ime for Takeoff), it is imperative that we pray Psalm 139:23-24. Remember, in order to **see** the Lord work amazing things, we need to consecrate ourselves **today**. We need to ask the Lord each morning to search us, test us, and examine our hearts to see if there is anything that will throw us off balance (A-lignment). The tendency for busy women (me included) is to hop on the front and start pedaling. But, too often we find ourselves pedaling from the front seat, gripping the handlebars of control while dragging all the extra weight behind. This is not what the instruction manual says. Do you remember week one, lesson one? The Captain has a reason for the tandem seating arrangement. He knows we can't steer AND pedal. Only He can. With God in the driver's seat, we can climb to heights we never thought possible.

> **N-ecessary Stops**
> **D-on't Stop Pedaling**

Let's review Matthew 11:28-30 and look at N-ecessary Stops and D-on't Stop Pedaling.

"Come to me, all you who are weary and burdened, and I will give you rest. Take my yoke upon you and learn from me, for I am gentle and humble in heart, and you will find rest for your souls. For my yoke is easy and my burden is light." Matthew 11:28-30

In light of Riding Tandem, how does Jesus encourage us to take N-ecessary Stops and D-on't Stop Pedaling?

_____

_____

_____

_____

_____

_____

Jesus says, "Come to me. I've got this! Don't rely on your own strength. If you keep pedaling in your own power, you will become weary and burdened. Take **N-ecessary Stops** and sit for a while. I can and will give you rest. **D-on't Stop Pedaling**. Don't give up. Learn from Me along the way. I am unlike the world that tells you to pedal faster and harder just to be noticed and valued. I love you just the way you are. Even in the fast pace of life, you can **E-njoy this Ride** because I am with you. I will be your strength, and I will never leave you to ride alone. Never. I am gentle. I am humble. I am here.

Come with me on this tandem journey,

E-njoy the Ride

We need to **E-njoy the Ride** God has for **us**. Just as every bike is different, God has designed each of us with a different purpose, passion, and provision. He will supply our every need, and we do not have to worry about the road ahead. We see this truth in Paul's tandem ride with Jesus.

Let's review and read Philippians 4:15-20 with a focus on Philippians 4:19.

What do you think it means that we are supplied with ALL of our needs through Jesus Christ?

> "My God will richly fill your every need in a glorious way through Christ Jesus."
>
> Philippians 4:19

_____

_____

While Paul is thanking the church in Philipi for contributing to his earthly needs, this verse (Philippians 4:19) shows us Paul's confidence in God to supply our EVERY NEED—earthly and spiritual. God will never leave us without His provision. He gives us the same glorious riches that He gave to His Son, Jesus. We can **E-njoy this Ride** because He **completely** takes care of us. In order to believe this and find rest for our souls, we need to:

- Take intentional **T-ime for Takeoff**
- **A-lign** ourselves with the Lord
- Know the **N-ecessary Stopping** points
- **D-on't Stop Pedaling** when life gets hard
- **E-njoy and Ride** and press on.

Isn't Riding Tandem with the Lord a fascinating concept? My prayer is that even when you finish this study, you will always be reminded of this simple acronym—T. A. N. D. E. M.

It's time to learn about **M-ark the Moments**—our final "hurrah" where we can celebrate ALL that God has shown us in this amazing study! To begin this week, I am going to share with you one of my favorite M-ark the Moments in Scripture. It's the foundation of my ministry ThouArtExalted (1 Chronicles 29:11, KJV).

Lets read together 1 Chronicles 29:1-20 (It's long but totally worth reading!)

What is the task? For whom is the temple being built? (1 Chronicles 29:1)

_____

_____

Who has provided for the construction of the temple? (1 Chronicles 29:2-5)

_____

_____

Why is David so overwhelmed with joy? (1 Chronicles 29:6-9)

_____

_____

What does David call the Lord in his prayer of overwhelming joy? (1 Chronicles 29:10-13)

_____

_____

How do you see David's humility? (1 Chronicles 29:14-16)

_____

_____

From where does our provision come? (1 Chronicles 29:14)

_____

_____

What happens when the people are so willing to give back to the Lord?

_____

_____

These verses are the pinnacle of **M-ark the Moment!** We see ALL the steps of Riding Tandem in David's actions. In the previous chapter, 1 Chronicles 28, David takes **T-ime for Takeoff** to understand his role in the building of the temple. David wanted to build it, but because he was a "warrior and had shed blood," the job was designed for his son, Solomon. Instead of having a pity-party, David **A-ligned** himself with the will of God and took action to prepare Solomon's heart to wholeheartedly follow after the Lord (1 Chronicles 28:9-10). David took the **N-ecessary Stops** to give Solomon all the plans the Holy Spirit had given him down to the very last detail (1 Chronicles 28:11-19). David **Never Stopped Pedaling** as he not only gave out of his personal treasures to build the temple, but also appealed to the people to give from their hearts. We arrive at the highlight of the event where ALL the people of Israel are **E-njoying the Ride** because of their overflowing love and generosity. We can **M-ark this Moment** in history because ALL was provided to build the temple, and God alone was glorified! WOW!

Did you notice David's question in 1 Chronicles 29:5? I hope this stirred something in your heart from last week's lesson!

"Now, who is willing to **consecrate** themselves to the LORD today?" 1 Chronicles 29:5

Why is this amazing? Because this is the same word we looked at last week—**consecrate.**

Joshua told the people, "**Consecrate** yourselves, for tomorrow the LORD will do amazing things among you." Joshua 1:5

Consecrate. Purify. Set yourself apart for the Lord. Get on the back of the tandem (I am sure that's what consecrate means in Hebrew!) for tomorrow you will see His wonders! I love when we get to **see** (uncover, reveal) a golden thread through Scripture.

I hope you are getting the idea of what it means to M-ark the Moment. It's the perfect way to end our ride together rejoicing in ALL that God did and continues to do for us—in the small moments where no one is watching, as well as the BIG moments for all to see. This week, we will be looking at M-arking Moments where we can **see** the acronym of Riding Tandem and the hand of God—both from our lives and in the pages of Scripture. Its going to be so exciting!

Yesterday we saw the incredible joy and generosity that comes when we believe ALL we have is from God and for God.

When we live in this mindset, we are able to enjoy this tandem ride and **M-ark the special moments** when God shows Himself to us in personal ways.

Two years ago, my daughter worked at Crooked Creek, a Young Life camp in Colorado. She was on the summer wait staff where she served more than 800 campers three meals a day. While she had to get up e-a-r-l-y to set up for breakfast, Daley's leaders also made it a priority for them to have a quiet time before they rode through their day. She e-mailed me in delight with this passage from Luke 4:40.

> "When the sun was setting, the people brought to Jesus all who had various kinds of sickness, and laying his hands on **each one,** he healed them."

"Mom," she said, "I can bring my heart, my experiences, and my disappointments all to Jesus and **one-by-one,** He can heal me, too."

This was not only a moment marker for Daley, but also for me. When I pray for my children's faith, I pray for them to know Jesus intimately. Daley, at 15, had discovered Jesus in a personal way. It wasn't my faith, her dad's faith, or her friends' faith. It became hers alone. She was taking the time to prepare her heart (T-ime for Takeoff) and allow the Captain to steady her bike (A-lignment). She was learning to take stops when needed (N-ecessary Stops) and press on through long days (D-on't Stop Pedaling). She was E-njoying the Ride because she was seeing firsthand how Scripture can tandem with personal experience. Daley was allowing her stories to intertwine with the Word that is holy and true. The result? An authentic faith that **propels more trust** to believe, and love, and give, and serve, and tell others about the Captain of her life—ALL with a thankful heart. She was **M-arking the Moment** and mine, too.

> "One by one he placed his hands on them and healed them."
>
> Luke 4:40 (MSG)

Let's look at a passage in Scripture where another woman's faith becomes personal.

Read John 4:4-26. I pray that even though you may know this passage well, it will be a new M-arking Moment.

What initial question did Jesus ask the Samaritan woman? (John 4:7)

_____

_____

What was her answer? (John 4:9)

_____

_____

What did Jesus know about this woman? Did it stop Him from telling her the truth? (John 4:18)

_____

_____

At what point in the story do you think the Samaritan woman had a marking moment?

_____

_____

Read John 4:27-42.

What happened because of this woman's belief in Jesus?

_____

_____

How did she give marking moments to others in the town? How did their faith become personal, like Daley's? (John 4:42)

_____

_____

I'm curious to see where you put the Samaritan's M-ark the Moment turnaround. Was it when Jesus revealed her past? Was it when Jesus declared He was the Messiah? I'm sure the whole day was a M-ark the Moment in and of itself, but I believe her moment was the initial **invitation** to get Him some water. Jesus, a man and a Jew, should never have been talking to a woman in the first place, let alone a Samaritan with a not-so-good reputation. He met her in her everyday world and invited her into His Kingdom. Her gender, her class, and how many times she had been married did not matter. Jesus loved her as He loves us—**abundantly** and without judgement. We are ALL His children, and we are ALL invited to ride one-on-one with the King of all Kings. This invitation was the beginning of a new ride and a chance to be forgiven and leave the past behind. Jesus did not sugar coat her current situation, but He extended her **grace.** I have written this note in my Bible: What is it about Jesus that allows Him to protect my dignity even when He exposes my sin?

Let's read 2 Corinthians 5:14-21.

How is it possible that we are a new creation in Christ?

_____

_____

_____

_____

What do you think is the ministry of reconciliation?

_____

_____

_____

_____

What are we called in 2 Corinthians 5:20?

_____

_____

_____

The word for reconcile is to settle an account. Jesus settled the account of sin once and for all. We are all invited to be new creations in Christ. I like to call it the **New Creation Invitation!** I can remember my invitation like it was yesterday. Jesus met me, too, in a very low spot. He invited me to be a new creation, to understand my need for forgiveness, and to believe for all eternity that I can Ride Tandem with Him! He settled my sin account on the cross, and He settled yours, too. I love what the Samaritan woman did in response to her invitation. She **hurried** to the village to tell everyone about this man! The word spread and many came to believe that day.

An invitation to believe in Him leads to intimacy. Intimacy leads to tandem riding, and tandem riding leads to telling others **your story. Your testimony. Your M-ark the Moments.** Have you ever considered that your story could become someone else's invitation to know Jesus? As tandem riders, it is our mission to live the gospel and **hurry** to share the gospel. We are called to know Him and then to make Him known. The Samaritan woman made Him known that day.

As I type this, my computer keeps inviting me to upgrade to the newest software. Do you know what it is called?

El Capitan. (Yes, it's spelled right.) This reminds me that once we have accepted the initial invitation to ride with Jesus, He invites us everyday to upgrade our journey with Him. Upgrade our thoughts. Upgrade our praise. Upgrade our vision. Upgrade our actions. Upgrade our compassion. Upgrade our trust. Upgrade our passion to share Jesus with others.

I want to close with 2 Corinthians 5:14-15.

"For Christ's love **compels** us, because we are convinced that one died for all, and therefore all died. And he died for all, that those who live should no longer live for themselves but for him who died for them and was raised again." 2 Corinthians 5:14,15

Are you compelled by Christ's love? Are you convinced that Jesus died once and for all for your sin? What areas in your life do you need to upgrade to El Capitan? It's **never** too late. Luke 4:40 tells us that WHILE THE SUN WAS SETTING, Jesus laid His hands on them and healed them **one-by-one**. It doesn't matter where you are on your journey, as long as you receive, open, and RSVP to the invitation. Yes, Lord. I accept with pleasure your kind invitation to make me a new creation! (My southern mom would be so proud!) What a special day. Thank you for your honesty. Jesus will meet you right where you are hurting and need some upgrading. In a closing prayer, write down your M-ark the Moment when you received your New Creation Invitation or share the areas where you need upgrading. These are great moments to write down and remember. Amen.

_____
_____
_____
_____
_____
_____
_____
_____
_____
_____
_____
_____
_____
_____

Lesson Three / NOTHING IS IMPOSSIBLE

I love that we get to close our study with M-ark the Moments. It's almost as if we are closing with a journal of our journey together.

Today, we get to peek inside a story of sincerity and hope in the one and only Lord. It is a prayer that illustrates the sweetness of Riding Tandem. It is the journey of Mary, the mother of our Lord Jesus.

Read Luke 1:26-56.

Let's be creative today! I want you to identify where Mary rode tandem with the Lord's plans for her life. There are no right or wrong answers (or grading for that matter!). You don't have to go in order either. Have fun with this exercise, let the Holy Spirit be your breeze, and list your verses with each letter of T.A.N.D.E.M.

T-Time for Takeoff

_____
_____
_____
_____
_____

A-Alignment

_____
_____
_____
_____
_____

N-Necessary Stops

_____
_____
_____
_____
_____

D-Don't Stop Pedaling

_____
_____
_____
_____
_____

E-Enjoy the Ride

_____
_____
_____
_____

M-Mark the Moment

_____
_____
_____
_____
_____

I hope you enjoyed that assignment. I sure did! It's super exciting for me to apply **all** that we have learned these last six weeks to Scripture. This is a key aspect of Riding Tandem with the Lord—learning how He uses **our lives** to tandem personal experiences with the Word to teach us His truth. I just love it!

Here's what I see in Mary's journey. I see her preparation for **T-akeoff** happened long before the angel appeared. God saw her heart and knew before the creation of time that she would be highly favored and chosen as the one to carry the Savior into this world. Because of her strong Jewish foundation, Mary knew God personally and **A-ligned** herself to His will without much questioning. She was indeed greatly troubled (Luke 1:29) which means *diatarassō*. It sounds like the word distressed to me. I found it interesting that this word meaning to trouble greatly, or to throw into confusion[1] is only used ONCE in the New Testament. It is used to describe Mary's heart. Even afraid, Mary moved forward and surrendered to God's plan. It's a great lesson for all of us. My favorite depiction of Mary was illustrated by a kindergarten student at our school. The sketch was proportional except for Mary's eyes—they were as big as watermelons! When I saw it, I thought to myself, *"This picture is right on target!"* I would have been *diatarassō*, too!

Even afraid, Mary moved forward and surrendered to God's plan.

I also love that God gave her an immediate **N-ecessary Stop.** Knowing the culture of that day, she could have been stoned to death because she was pregnant before marriage. The angel told her to not be afraid and as a confirmation to the endless possibilities of God's power, even her barren cousin, Elizabeth, was pregnant at an old age.[2] Again, we see the word **hurry** as Mary went to visit her cousin, Elizabeth, where she was taken care of for three months. Mary **D-idn't Stop Pedaling** as she was obedient to being the Lord's servant. She was committed to the ride and stepped into the role of being the Messiah's mother, even though the future was scary and uncertain. Her song in Luke 1:46-56 is evidence that she was **E njoying the Ride.** Do you hear the joy?

> "My soul glorifies the Lord and my spirit rejoices in God my Savior, for he has been mindful of the humble state of his servant. From now on all generations will call me blessed, for the Mighty One has done great things for me—holy is his name. His mercy extends to those who fear him, from generation to generation." Luke 1:47-50

There are more **M-ark the Moments** than I can count! I am not sure I can choose one in particular. However, I loved that John the Baptist leaped inside of Elizabeth's womb when he "met" Jesus for the first time. I think this is so GOD! He allows us to take joy in the little things and mark them for glory! His glory!

Take JOY in the little things and Mark the Moments

As I write this lesson, today is my 21st wedding anniversary. Each anniversary, Curry and I have been taking turns surprising each other with a special trip. It doesn't have to be elaborate, but it is important to MARK IT. One year, Winnie was just three-weeks old and we **still** went away for the night. Just for the record, I'm not so sure I would have done this with my first-born. But by this time in motherhood, I knew Winnie wouldn't break, so I made the evening special with my husband. I gave Winnie to my mother-in-law, packed my pump, and took off. **Nothing is impossible.**

We need to **M-ark** the special God-given Moments in our lives. They may be anniversaries, births, weddings, or graduations. They can also be conversations, breakthroughs, fulfilled dreams, and even moments that aren't so easy. We must have our eyes open to see the Captain leading us through this life. We must have our hearts open to say, "I am the Lord's servant." We can M-ark the Moments and even better—**write them down** as Mary did.

Think of the little moments where God has met you this week. Celebrate this time with Him. Be joyful as you are filled with the promise that He will never leave you. Riding Tandem is a privilege. Lean into His leading today.

M-ark the special moments of your Riding Tandem journey with God this week.

_____
_____
_____
_____
_____
_____
_____
_____
_____
_____
_____
_____
_____
_____
_____
_____
_____
_____
_____
_____
_____
_____
_____
_____
_____
_____
_____
_____
_____

Lesson Four/ WHAT'S THE HURRY?

Yesterday, we concluded with the beginning of Mary's tandem journey and her beautiful heartfelt song of praise.

Today, I want to continue reading in Luke where we see the shepherd's response to the angels and the birth of Jesus.

Let's begin by reading Luke 2:15-20. (If you want to start from Luke 2:8, you will get a better background for our lesson today.)

What is the similarity between the shepherd's reaction and the Samaritan woman's reaction after they encountered Jesus? (Luke 2:16-17)

_____
_____
_____
_____

What was Mary's reaction to all the events? Why do you think this is significant?

_____
_____
_____

I love when we can connect the Scripture we are reading to other verses we have learned. I believe this is a work of the Holy Spirit. God's Word is alive and touches our hearts in different ways. When we are IN His Word often, we will see connections that will deepen our faith and enrich our tandem journey!

When both the Samaritan woman and the shepherds encountered Jesus, they felt an urgency to spread the word about their experience. Their personal interaction ignited (stoked) a passion for others to know Christ that still continues to have a ripple effect on our generation. When we read about personal encounters with Jesus in Scripture and heartfelt desires to share these experiences with others, we should be inspired to do the same. These M-ark the Moment times can be the inspiration for someone else's tandem journey to begin.

When was the last time you shared a personal encounter with Jesus with a friend? Did it ignite a passion for that person to want to know Jesus, too?

_____
_____
_____
_____
_____
_____

I lived in Honolulu, Hawaii the summer after my Junior year at SMU and worked at McDonalds. I was on a Campus for Christ Summer Project and our mission was to share the gospel of Jesus in a creative way on the beaches of Waikiki. Not a bad summer—except for the fact that I gave a cute Japanese girl a milk shake instead of a McChicken sandwich due to the language barrier. But my MARK the moment did not happen at Mickey D's nor while witnessing on the beach. It happened when I was on my way to the airport to pick up my parents who were coming to visit. There were two girls in the cab with me, and they asked me why I was in Hawaii. My heart just spilled out. It was not forced. It was not something I had to do. No one was watching. I honestly believe it was the first time I shared my love about Jesus in an authentic way. I will have no idea what ripple effect my testimony made on those two girls, but I **treasured** the moment—and marked it. It was the highlight of my whole nine-week experience. It even trumped the advancement from scooping lard into the french fry vat to taking orders at the window. Aloha, Annie.

Here's another M-ark the Moment connection from Luke 1:39 and Luke 2:16.

Read these passages and see if you can find the repeating word.

"At that time Mary got ready and **hurried** to a town in the hill country of Judea, . . ." Luke 1:39

"So they **hurried** off and found Mary and Joseph, and the baby, who was lying in the manger. " Luke 2:16

What are they hurrying off to do?

_____
_____
_____
_____

I hope you saw the word **hurried**. Riding Tandem has been about leaning into the leading of God, surrendering control, relaxing your grip, and allowing Him to steer at His pace and perfect timing. Now we see the word hurry. What on earth?

Both Mary and the shepherds had divine encounters and hurried off to seek the truth about their experiences. Mary hurried to be with Elizabeth and the shepherds hurried off to find the baby. They were **hurrying** to see if God's Word was truth. They both got their answer, too. Mary found Elizabeth was pregnant just as the angel had said, and the shepherds found the baby in a manger swaddled in cloths, just as the angel said. Do we have this hurry conviction to see God's truth at work? Do we get up in the morning with a desire to read Scripture and **see** where God is going to show up in our day? Do we hurry to live by the promises of God? Do we hurry to trust Him? If we do, then we will be marking this Scripture passage and finding peace in any moment.

Let's read Philippians 4:4-9.

> **What actions should we take to hurry to believe in God's promises? I will start us off. I see ten action verbs!**
>
> **1. Rejoice.**
> **2. Rejoice again.**
> **3. Be gentle and make evident for all to SEE.**
> **4.** _____
> **5.** _____
> **6.** _____
> **7.** _____
> **8.** _____
> **9.** _____
> **10.** _____

> **What are the promises from these verses? Again, I will start us off.**
>
> **1. The Lord is near.**
> **2. The peace of God will guard your heart in Jesus.**
> **3.** _____
> **4.** _____

When we **hurry** to see God, there is an urgency to put His promises into practice. Once we do, we will be able to M-ark many special moments and see Him actively work in our lives. We will encounter the living Christ in a personal way and our stories will have a **ripple effect** for the Kingdom. Too often, we hurry to take control, hurry for the next event, and hurry to see things done in our way and in our own timing. Today, let's hurry to see Jesus. Let's open our eyes and see His wonders. Let's tell our story. To close our lesson, here is one of my favorite songs by Big Daddy Weave. Listen to these lyrics.

> If I told you my story,
> You would hear hope that wouldn't let go
> and if I told you my story,
> you would hear Love that never gave up
> and if I told you my story,
> you would hear Life, but it wasn't mine
>
> If I should speak, then let it be of the grace
> that is Greater than all my sin
> If I should speak let it be of the grace that is Greater
> than all my sin
> of when justice was served, and where mercy wins!
> of the kindness of Jesus, that draws me in[3]

Dear Lord, thank You for giving me a story to tell. I pray today I would be in a hurry to study the truth of Your Word, so I can share the story of hope, victory, love, and life. You know everything about me. You will see me to the mountain tops high, as well as the valleys low. You are my lead, and I will follow You with wholehearted devotion. Thank You for giving us the Bible about stories of encounters with Jesus that continue to inspire us today. Let my story and my testimony be used to invite someone else to Ride Tandem with You. Amen.

Did I just type lesson five, week six? That's just amazing. Do you remember how we started our journey together?

If you look back to week one, lesson one, you will see that we received a tandem bicycle with a letter from our Captain. Since we have studied six weeks in Riding Tandem together, I want to see if reading these instructions will put a smile on your face.

Welcome! Let Me Introduce Myself. My name is Captain, and I am overjoyed that you chose Me to ride through life with you. We are going to take amazing adventures together. As your Captain, I know the direction we will take. There's no need to be distracted by all the latest gadgets and gizmos because I have all the equipment you need. I have plenty of water, and rest stops are planned well in advance. If you ever feel tired, insecure, or winded, just stop pedaling and coast. I have you in the palm of My hand. If you ever get scared, worried, or doubt My leading, just lean in and trust that I am steering you in the right direction. Make sure to mark the special moments we will have together and always remember to enjoy the ride. Life can get tricky sometimes, but if you trust Me, I will give you eyes to see from My perspective. Do not worry. As your Captain, I am in full control. Before you climb aboard, please read My instructions and know your seating assignment. It is very important to know our takeoff procedures before we ride together on this tandem bicycle.

With everlasting love,
Your Captain

This letter reminds me of reading a brochure before you go on a trip. We won't experience the fullness of the trip unless we experience the journey first hand. Now, we can look back at this instruction manual and say, "Ah, yes. I know **by experience** that my Captain and I will take amazing adventures together. He helps me know when to ride, when to coast, and when to stop altogether. He knows the importance of my T-akeoff procedures, my A-lignment, my N-ecessary Stops, my pressing on through difficulty, my ability to E-njoy the Ride, and my special M-ark the Moments together with Him. All of these help me see His glory and hurry to speak about His promises."

As we close our study together, we are going to look closely at two Scriptures that "tandem" together in a beautiful way. Both mark moments in their own way, but **together are powerful** and applicable to our final journey in Riding Tandem.

First, let's look at a Scripture and a question I asked you yesterday. We barely skimmed the surface of its depth.

What's was Mary's response to all that was happening to her in Luke 2:19?

_____

_____

_____

The word I want us to mark is the word **treasured.** This word is translated from the Greek word "tereo" meaning to guard. Treasured is syn**tereo** meaning to keep safe, to preserve.[4] Mary was M-arking the Moment by **guarding** this special moment entrusted to her—a moment that marked all history.

In tandem with this verse, let's read Genesis 15:1-11.

What were the first words the Lord said to Abram in his vision? (Genesis 15:1)

_____

_____

What was promised or entrusted to Abram? (Genesis 15:4-5, 7)

_____

_____

What did Abram have to do to M-ark the Moment of the covenant? (Genesis 15:9-10)

_____

_____

What specifically happens in Genesis 15:11, and what is Abram's reaction?

_____

_____

The Lord made a covenant with Abram and promised him a line of offspring that would lead to the birth of the Messiah, Jesus Christ. What I find interesting is a quick line in Scripture we might miss. Stay with me.

"Then birds of prey came down on the carcasses, but Abram drove them away." Genesis 15:11

Once the sacrifice was cut in half, Abram had to **protect** it from birds of prey. He had **to guard what was entrusted to Him.** Can you see the connection? In both cases, Abram and Mary were believing in God's promises on extreme levels. Both were making sacrifices. Both were treasuring. Both were protecting and **guarding** the covenant promise. Abram was on the front end of the promise while Mary was seeing the promise come to life right before her eyes. Because of Abram's determination to guard the covenant, Mary treasured one of God's richest M-ark the Moments of all history—the birth of Jesus Christ.

I believe we can take these two experiences and apply them into our lives as well—Our M-ark the Moments. Why? Because we, too, need to **protect the gospel** and **our tandem times with God**. The enemy is still sending birds of prey to destroy the promises God has placed in our hearts. Just think about marriage, for example. Oh, the enemy is good at this one. I know by experience that after 21 years, you can look at each other as simple business partners if you don't purposefully protect, treasure, and guard your covenant to each other. It takes a lot of hard work and sacrifice.

What about you? Identify a M-ark the Moment. Next, identify how the enemy might have another plan to steal that moment.

_____

_____

_____

What weapon are you going to use to protect your tandem journey with God?

_____

_____

_____

When we have our M-ark the Moments, we need to remember to protect what God has entrusted to us. Birds of prey are pesky! They come in many forms: doubt, fear, impatience, anger, bitterness, or disappointment. It's our job to protect our Riding Tandem. We cannot be negligent. We have to do our work.

Look up the following Scripture. What are we to GUARD?

• **Psalm 141:3**

_____

_____

- **Proverbs 4:13, 23**

_____

_____

- **Proverbs 7:2**

_____

_____

- **Luke 12:15**

_____

_____

- **2 Timothy 1:14**

"Through the power of the Holy Spirit who lives within us, carefully guard the precious truth that has been entrusted to you." 2 Timothy 1:14 (NLT)

_____

_____

- **1 John 5:21**

"Dear children, keep away from anything that might take God's place in your hearts." 1 John 5:21 (NLT)

_____

_____

I think this is the perfect way to end our journey together. In order to Ride Tandem, we have to take this relationship with Jesus **seriously**. We have to **treasure** ALL the blessings God has given to us, and we have to **protect** them.

> We have to **guard** what we say to one another.
> We have to **guard** our hearts and God's teachings.
> We have to **guard** against false teachings and all kinds of evil.
> We have to **guard** our minds, our souls, and all our ways.
> We have to **carefully guard** the PRECIOUS TRUTH that has been entrusted to us.

We have been given so much to treasure. The list is too long to recite. The NASB version of 2 Timothy 1:14 says

"Guard, through the Holy Spirit who dwells in us, the treasure which has been entrusted to you."

We have to guard the treasure we have been given.

How are you going to treasure your journey with God? Have you seen a difference in your walk with Jesus as a result of Riding T-A-N-D-E-M? Share your thoughts.

T-Time for Takeoff

_____

_____

_____

_____

A-Alignment

_____
_____
_____
_____
_____
_____

N-Necessary Stops

_____
_____
_____
_____
_____
_____

D-Don't Stop Pedaling

_____
_____
_____
_____
_____
_____

E-Enjoy the Ride

_____
_____
_____
_____
_____
_____

M-Mark the Moments

_____
_____
_____
_____
_____
_____

Oh, I wish I could see how Riding Tandem has blessed your journey with Jesus. Allow me to share a few testimonies from special friends. I know they will be encouraging to you.

Thank You, Lord, for being my Captain. It has been and will continue to be the ride of a lifetime. I love how You steady our bike each morning, and how You wait so patiently for me to take the rear position. I am so grateful that You steer our bike through the day. It gives me much more of an opportunity to enjoy the ride and to see things from a different perspective. When there is a hill up ahead that seems impossible to climb, I know that I can trust You to give me the extra power to get to the top. We always make it together. When we make it to the summit, what a view there is to be seen! I especially love the times when we can take a break from riding altogether and just sit and talk by the river. I love spending time with You like that. Thank You, Jesus, for teaching me how to ride this tandem bike with You. I now have the balance to ride hands free! -Evelyn Viana

Lord, thank You for inviting me to ride with You on this tandem bike. I repent for trying to sit in the front Captain's seat, and I ask for Your forgiveness. Thank You for allowing me to pedal in sync with YOUR rhythm and steering. Your leading is fascinating, and one I don't always understand from the back seat. But I do know that You love me and I love You—so trust seems to be making sense of it all. -Nike Whittemore

For so long, I took the lead operating on my own strength and wisdom, only to find myself exhausted, burnt-out, and completely lost. Yet You continue to love me despite my stubbornness. Today, as I dust myself off, I surrender my pain, suffering, and regrets from the past. I fully acknowledge that these feelings and thoughts will only keep me off my course. I release all control and invite You back into the "Captain" seat. Lord, I trust in You to lead, for You God, know the beginning to the end. Thank You Lord for all provision, protection, and strength through Your presence. Amen -Marie Levesque

Lord, I thank You for this tandem bike ride You have planned just for me. I pray that each morning I would hop on the back humbly surrendering control to You and seeking You above all things so that I will see what You want me to see. Help me to fan the flames of my gifts to fulfill Your purposes. Help me also to be prayerful, watchful, and thankful and to be aware of the things that draw me out of alignment with You. I pray that when You stop the ride I would use the time to realign myself with You and that when times are hard I would fight with uncommon weapons like trust, mercy, and patience. Keep the fruit in my heart good so that I can live a JOY-filled life remembering that true joy comes only from You. Remind me to mark, treasure, and protect my moments with You so that someday those moments, when connected, will show a life lived to glorify You. Amen! -Lindsey Riggs

For a Bible study I thought I did not have time for, I am so grateful that the Holy Spirit did not let me go so easily. I am almost crying as I type this because God is so good to meet us right where I need Him. I think I am the most grateful that I have written down this verse:

Lord, search Amy and know her heart. Test me and know my anxious thoughts. See if there is any offensive way in me and lead me in the way of everlasting ~ Psalm 139:23-24

I need to re-align my heart every day and get off that front seat. Even though I like to decorate my bike with streamers and hot pink reflection lights, a mounted cell phone holder and coffee cup wired on, saddle bags etc, -He still needs to be the driver, and I am tired of driving. It's time to trust and throw my hands out. I am so blessed to have a Father in Heaven who loves me like this. -Amy Franks

Now it's your turn . . . Yes, YOU. We have ridden SIX weeks together. Write a prayer to your Captain and thank Him for this journey to Ride Tandem.

_____
_____
_____
_____
_____
_____
_____
_____
_____
_____
_____
_____
_____
_____
_____
_____
_____
_____
_____
_____
_____
_____
_____
_____
_____
_____
_____
_____
_____
_____
_____
_____

I , for one, treasure **you** and the time spent together on this Riding Tandem adventure. My prayer is that we would not forget our journey together. Just as God used the visual of the stars to show Abram how many descendents he would have, we have the visual of the tandem bike to realign us with the purposes God has for us. We have the tandem to remind us to view life from the back seat knowing that God is in control at ALL times. He knows what's ahead and will give us all the strength, endurance, equipment, and patience we need to handle life. We need to stop pedaling at times to coast. We need to keep pedaling at times to run this race with perseverance. We need to remember to enjoy life and mark moments where God shows up. Oh, the glory of knowing Jesus.

Treasure this journey.

Receive the invitation today and enjoy the ride of your life.

I love you dearly.

Annie

Our TANDEM journey:

T- _____ for Takeoff.
A- _____.
N- _____ Stops.
D- _____ Stop Pedaling.
E- _____ the Ride.
M- _____ the Moments.

Jesus' love compels us to believe, love, and serve.
This is the **power** of the resurrection.

> "The Spirit of God, who raised Jesus from the dead, lives in you. And just as God raised Christ Jesus from the dead, he will give life to your mortal bodies by this same Spirit living within you."
>
> Romans 8:11
> (NLT)

Riding Tandem is all about a _____.

To proclaim our Tandem Journey, we need to tell our _____.

Answers: time, alignment, necessary, don't, enjoy, mark, relationship, stories

CHAPTER ONE:
1. Definition of kyrios, http://www.blueletterbible.org/lang/lexicon/lexicon.cfm?Strongs=G2962&t=KJV
2. Definition of kyrios, http://en.wikipedia.org/wiki/Kyrios
3. Definition of stoker, http://www.definitions.net/definition/Stoker
4. Fan into flames, http://www.blueletterbible.org/lang/lexicon/lexicon.cfm?Strongs=G329&t=KJV
5. Definition of to know, yada, http://www.blueletterbible.org/lang/lexicon/lexicon.cfm?Strongs=H3045&t=KJV
6. Definition of pala, https://www.blueletterbible.org/lang/lexicon/lexicon.cfm?Strongs=H6381&t=NKJV

CHAPTER TWO:
1. http://business-finance.blurtit.com/3171446/what-does-duracell-say-about-the-durability-of-their-brand
2. Sarah Young, *Jesus Calling*, (Nashville, Tennessee, Thomas Nelson Publishing, ©2004), February 10th, pg. 43
3. http://www.merriam-webster.com/dictionary/aligned?show=0&t=1414099269
4. Major W. Ian Thomas, *The Saving Life of Christ*, (Grand Rapids, Michigan, Zondervan Publishing, ©1961)
5. Definition of *devotion*: https://www.blueletterbible.org/lang/lexicon/lexicon.cfm?Strongs=G4342&t=KJV
6. Definition of *watch*: https://www.blueletterbible.org/lang/lexicon/lexicon.cfm?Strongs=G1127&t=KJV
7. NIV Study Bible, Zondervan, Proverbs 28:26, Footnote: pg. 986
8. Major W. Ian Thomas, *The Saving Life of Christ*, (Grand Rapids, Michigan, Zondervan Publishing, ©1961). pg. 23,24
9. Major W. Ian Thomas, *The Saving Life of Christ*, (Grand Rapids, Michigan, Zondervan Publishing, ©1961). pg. 19
10. Definition of reveal: https://www.blueletterbible.org/lang/lexicon/lexicon.cfm?Strongs=G601&t=KJV
11. Yawhy: http://www.blueletterbible.org/lang/lexicon/lexicon.cfm?Strongs=H136&t=NASB
12. Jehovah: http://www.blueletterbible.org/lang/lexicon/lexicon.cfm?Strongs=H3068&t=NASB
13. Definition of see: http://www.blueletterbible.org/lang/lexicon/lexicon.cfm?Strongs=H1540&t=KJV

CHAPTER THREE:
1. The Days of Heaven Upon Earth, *Steams in the Desert*, (Grand Rapids, Michigan, Zondervan, Copyright 1925), pg. 198
2. Definition of Nathan: http://www.blueletterbible.org/lang/lexicon/lexicon.cfm?Strongs=H5414&t=KJV
3. Lauren Daigle, *Trust in You*, Published by Lyrics © Sony/ATV Music Publishing LLC ©2015
4. John Eldridge, *Ransomed Heart: Daily Devotional*, September 30th, © Copyright RANSOMED HEART MINISTRIES.
5. Casting Crowns, *The Voice of Truth*, ©2003 Beach Street Records

CHAPTER FOUR:
1. Definition of *Darak,* https://www.blueletterbible.org/lang/lexicon/lexicon.cfm?Strongs=H1869&t=KJV
2. http://healthyliving.azcentral.com/bicycle-built-two-work-7507.html
3. Drive Train: https://en.wikipedia.org/wiki/Chain_drive
4. http://biblehub.com/commentaries/pulpit/matthew/27.htm
5. http://tonyevans.org/mobile/the-confidence-of-faith/
6. A.B. Simpson, *Steams in the Desert*, (Grand Rapids, Michigan, Zondervan, Copyright 1925), pg. 148
7. Casting Crowns, *Hold it All Together*, ©2016 Beach Street Records

CHAPTER FIVE:
1. Definition of *Kuwn*, https://www.blueletterbible.org/lang/lexicon/lexicon.cfm?Strongs=H3559&t=NIV
2. Definition of *Quwm*, https://www.blueletterbible.org/lang/lexicon/lexicon.cfm?Strongs=H6965&t=NIV
3. Mark Batterson, *Draw the Circle: The 40 Day Prayer Challenge*, (Grand Rapids, Michigan, Zondervan, ©2012), pg. 24
4. Definition of sanctify, www.blueletterbible.org/lang/lexicon/lexicon.cfm?Strongs=H6942&t=NIV
5. J. Danson Smith, *Sit Still*, http://www.cobblestoneroadadministry.org/2005_CRM/Poem_SitStillByJDansonSmith.html
6. Sarah Young, *Jesus Calling*, (Nashville, Tennessee, Thomas Nelson Publishing, ©2004), February 10th, pg. 236

CHAPTER SIX:
1. Definition of diatarassō, https://www.blueletterbible.org/lang/lexicon/lexicon.cfm?Strongs=G1298&t=NIV
2. http://studybible.info/vines/Trouble%20(Noun%20and%20Verb)
3. Big Daddy Weave, My Story, Beautiful Offerings, Publishing: © 2015 Word Music, LLC, Weave Country (ASCAP) / Sony/ATV Music Publishing LLC, Open Hands Music (SESAC)
4. Definition of *syntereo*: https://www.blueletterbible.org/lang/lexicon/lexicon.cfm?Strongs=G4933&t=NIV

Annie Pajcic lives in Jacksonville, Florida with her husband and four children. Using her background in youth ministry, art, and graphic design, she started ThouArtExalted in 2007. ThouArtExalted is a non-profit 501(c)(3) ministry inspiring women and girls to live creatively for Christ. When Annie doesn't have paint on her hands, she is writing and designing Bible studies, picking up kids, cooking dinner, or feeding the chickens. Visit her website at **www. thouartexalted.com** for speaking engagements, art ideas, Bible studies, service projects, and devotionals.

SPECIAL THANKS!

I'm so thankful for the study of Riding Tandem. God has taken me through many N-ecessary Stops being a wife and a mom of four (not to mention a few A-lignments!). Jesus is so faithful, and I praise Him for creatively equipping me with His Word. A special thanks to my sweet co-captain, Curry, for his continued encouragement and "way-to-gos!" A BIG SHOUT out to: my amazing board, Joani and Ann, Leah Frye and Brooks Wilder for photography, Heather Stoll for tireless edits, Kevin, Eric, and Mark of CollabCreation film production, and sweet Mycah for an unending gracious spirit. Thank You, Jesus, for being my Captain and inviting me to ride with You. The journey is thrilling, humbling, and most of all rewarding. Until we see you face to face, let's ride on into eternity. Amen.

Riding Tandem for GIRLS!

* **12 Week Bible Study**

* Art Projects
* Journal Questions
* Memory Cards
* Recipes
* Service Projects

Riding Tandem for GIRLS: Leaning into the Leading of God is about an authentic, one-on-one relationship with God. It's about learning our position on the back of the bike and trusting God with the front steering. Our personal relationship with God is built for two. He is the Captain, and we must learn to lean into His leading, pedal forward, and trust Him with the directions.

Riding Tandem will teach us that while our final destination is heaven, our destiny on earth has purpose. It's an exciting adventure! We are not just along for the ride. God wants us to live an abundant life fully surrendered to His leading. Riding Tandem with Jesus is letting go of the handlebars and experiencing His power as we pedal. Everyday.

Using the imagery of the tandem bicycle, Riding Tandem is divided into twelve chapters using the acronym T-A-N-D-E-M to take us through our lessons: T-ime for Takeoff. A-lignment. N-ecessary Stops. D-on't Stop Pedaling. E-njoy the Ride. M-ark the Moments.

It's a beautiful day for a bike ride!

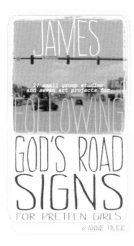

James/Following God's Road Signs: One Year Curriculum for Pre-teen/Teen Girls and Boys

James: Following God's Road Signs is a 27-week Bible study on the book of James for Middle School girls and boys. It is written to encourage and deepen faith when life isn't quite so easy. God is on our side and gives us INSTRUCTIONS for how to navigate—even when we choose to drive our own way. The book of James is a **road map** guiding us in the right direction. *Following God's Road Signs* teaches us to put our FAITH INTO ACTION by stopping, looking at God's map, and asking Him for directions. This study is great for youth groups, small groups, and homeschool groups.

What You Get:

- The book of James verse-by-verse in a fun, creative way
- 27 exciting Bible lessons
- **Creative art projects**
- Dig-deep discussion questions
- Lessons come in a **Digital PDF** format for easy sharing

ARTBox in your INBox: Twelve Month Digital Devotional with Art Projects for Pre-teen/Teen Girls

ARTBox in Your INBox was developed with pre-teen and teenage girls in mind. ARTBox is a creative devotional lesson that comes directly to your inbox **each month**. This new digital resource offers girls the chance to study God's Word and deepen their relationship with Jesus. ARTBox is also filled with fun art projects, memory verses, recipes, community service ideas, and more!

Each issue of ARTBox in Your INBox offers:

- 12 monthly PDF devotional lessons with real-life application
- FUN and CREATIVE art projects that reinforce Scripture
- Scripture memory verses
- Additional creative activities such as recipes, community service projects, conversation starters, Christian music play lists, and more

PLANTED is a ten-week **Women's Bible study** on Psalm 1:1-3. The study teaches us how to give up control and let God PLANT us where we need to be—so we can grow UP into the strong tree described in Psalm 1:2-3. When our roots are deeply PLANTED into the fellowship, the love, the grace, and the Word of God, we can't help but become a beautiful strong tree with purpose. Our leaves will not wither under the stresses and storms of life, our fruit will be abundant, and our lives will prosper! It's a promise on which we can stand.

- Workbook and 11 Teaching Videos available

He Knows My Name 20/20 Mini Lessons for Girls is a Bible study for middle school girls ages 10-14 based on John 10:3. Jesus is our Good Shepherd and we, His children, are the sheep of His pasture. Using the imagery of sheep and shepherds, He Knows My Name teaches girls that God will always love, protect, and lead into safe pastures. This study also includes five art projects connecting the story of the Good Shepherd into a creative form. Whether used in a personal devotion or a small group setting, the lessons are designed to take about 20 minutes.

What you Get:

- Engaging lesson plans about 20 minutes
- Extra Scripture to dig deeper
- Prayers for each lesson
- Personal application

5 Creative Art Projects

For Tween and Teen girls
ThouArtExalted Ministries

ThouArtExalted Ministry APP is a FREE devotional app for tween and teen girls to read through the New Testament in ONE YEAR! Each day they will receive a quick devotional right to their phones that will highlight verses from each chapter of the New Testament starting with Matthew. Packed with fun downloadable graphics, journal questions, prayers, and personal applications. Download here:
http://get.theapp.co/998f/

Visit WWW.THOUARTEXALTED.COM for more information